How to Choose a State Secondary School

A Complete Guide to Choosing the Right School for your Child

MIRANDA PERRY

THE OLEANDER PRESS

CAMBRIDGE

*How to Choose
a State
Secondary School*

The Oleander Press Ltd
16 Orchard Street
Cambridge
CB1 1JT
England

© 2006 Miranda Perry

ISBN 978 0906672 570

Typeset, printed and bound in Great Britain

Preface

Why All Parents Need this Guide

The choice of your child's secondary school is arguably one of the most important decisions you will have to make on their behalf. Success at school can bring great rewards in adulthood. There is a common consensus that 'doing well' at school usually results in 'doing well' in life, and every parent wants their child to have a bright future. Many of us are scarred by memories of difficult times at school ourselves and want our children to avoid similar experiences. Some parents regret their own lack of academic achievement and do not want their children to make the same mistakes.

But finding the right secondary school is a difficult process, not helped by regular scare stories in the media about substandard schools. There is a lot of misinformation about the nature of state secondary schools. It amazes me how the knowledge of many who comment on education amounts to little more than having gone to school themselves. I have heard journalists and politicians voice strong opinions on state education without ever having attended, and rarely been in, a state school. Parents then are often forced to make this important decision about their child's future, without very much quality evidence on which to rely.

Parents often take drastic steps to access their preferred school, sometimes spending more on a new house in a school's catchment area than private education would have cost them; or children travel distances to school further than their parents would tolerate for their own commute.

But these steps are often ill-advised. For example, I have found that parents might choose a school because of a reputation that could well be years out of date. Or they favour a school because it is oversubscribed, when the justifications for the oversubscription are long since gone. A school which suits one child might not be right for another. Children are individual and unique, as are schools, and their needs should be matched to what a school can offer.

This book attempts to give clear advice that will help parents make an informed decision as to the secondary state school that is right for their child. I aim to fill the vacuum of information and evidence that surrounds the issue of choosing a secondary school. I explain what sources of information are currently available, and how to interpret them. I outline the actions that parents can take to give themselves as full and complete a picture as possible of the secondary schools that are available to their child.

Why Me

I have criticised commentators whom I feel do not have the knowledge base to back up their opinions. It goes without saying then that I consider myself to be in a better position to comment. I have taught in a variety of state schools at different leadership levels for 13 years, have had experience of working in the independent sector and am currently an education adviser for a local education authority. I could be viewed as a successful product of state schooling myself, having attended a state comprehensive, Cambridge University, and then trained to be a teacher.

As this is a book purporting to give advice, I have endeavoured to be as objective as possible. However, I think it is only fair that I admit to some bias that will be all too evident despite my attempts at objectivity. I have been educated and have taught in state schools and am I am an advocate of them. I am convinced that state schools often provide a better education than the independent sector and it is this conviction that underpins everything contained in this book. I believe that being better informed about secondary education, rather than withdrawing from the state system altogether, is the course of action most likely to ensure your child goes to the right school.

If you would like to let me know about your own experiences of choosing a state secondary school, please contact me via the publisher, editor@oleanderpress.com.

How to Use this Guide

The book is split into four chapters which are broken down into bite-size sections.

You can work through the book from chapter 1 'The Choice' to chapter 4 'The Application', dip into particular, bullet pointed sections or use it as a guide when visiting schools, making enquiries, or researching. Each chapter links to the others, but can also stand alone.

The four chapters are then divided into short, accessible sections which include:

- an introduction
- a summary
- cross referencing with the glossary
- guidance on where to go for further information

Some sections have:

- a short case study illustrating the issue
- Easy Guides with key information sources annotated

Guide to Symbols and References

Words in the glossary are asterisked* the first time they appear in each section.

The guide makes clear if an issue is *a cause for concern* for parents by writing this phrase in italics.

Contents

Chapter 1 – The Choice

Introduction

This book focuses on state secondary comprehensive* schools in England. The majority of secondary schools start at Year 7* with pupils aged 11, however in a few areas of the country there are state selective grammar schools, and high schools which start at Year 9 with pupils aged 13.

This chapter describes some of the differences in secondary schools that might influence the choice of school for your child. The different types of school are listed in alphabetical order.

If you are in an area of high schools please refer to the chapter on middle/high schools and otherwise read Year 9 for Year 7.

Academies

At the time of writing, the development of academy schools* is a key component of the government's education policy. The first academy opened in 2002 and it is the government's aim to increase the number of academy schools from 27 at the time of writing to 200 by 2010. Academies are state schools but have a private sponsor who, in return for their contribution, has a significant degree of influence over the school's curriculum, ethos and staffing. Opinions differ as to the success of the new academies.

- A recent government-backed report found that seven out of eleven academies looked at had improved their Key Stage 4* results.
- The report highlighted several areas of concern: poor pupil discipline, bullying, badly designed buildings and high levels of exclusions.
- Academies are often opened to replace schools which were deemed as failing, according to Ofsted*.
- Because some academies have replaced failing schools, when they do publish results they often come quite low in the Achievement and Assessment Tables*. However, some academies are establishing a good improvement record for exam results and adding value*.
- There is no evidence yet to suggest academies are better than other state schools. Some academies have received negative Ofsted reports.
- Academies do not have to follow the National Curriculum*, and therefore have the flexibility to develop a curriculum that directly meets the needs of their students.
- Academies are often situated in areas of high deprivation but increasingly this is not reflected in their student intake.
- A large number of academies are sponsored by

religious groups and therefore have a religious ethos.

- Academies have their own admissions* criteria, although they have to abide by national guidelines. Parents therefore have to apply directly to academies, rather than through their LEA*.
- Academies are usually more popular with parents than the schools they replaced.
- Academies can select 10% of their students by aptitude.

Further Information
LEA
You can find out from your local education authority whether there are academy schools, or any plans to establish one, in your area.

To sum up:
The 'jury is out' as to the success of academies, and it is therefore necessary to research them with the same vigour that you would non-academy schools.

Extended Schools

Extended schools* offer extended services in addition to the main curriculum. A full extended school will offer childcare from 8.00am–6.00pm all year round, a range of extra-curricular activities, parenting support, and access for community activities. It will also have strong connections with the health service and social services.

By 2010, the government wants all schools to be full extended schools. At the time of writing most schools offer some extended services, a small number are full extended schools.

A school with extended services can:

- sometimes be attractive to students who are normally wary of school. This is because it might offer lots of additional provision the young person might be interested in, like an after school on site youth club.
- have a genuine community atmosphere to it, because it is a hub of activity for a variety of local people.
- provide a holistic education for a child, because of its range of services. It can make it easier for students to link what they are learning to the outside world.
- often be vibrantly multi-cultural, by attracting groups from the community who would otherwise not use the school.
- give students a wide range of services. There could be health practitioners on site, counsellors, careers advisers and youth workers.
- give students easier access to learning. There might be an after school club to support students' homework, or a breakfast club in the library.
- potentially give young people a more creative offer than a non-extended neighbour. There could be many activities that are not curriculum focused for young people to become involved in, for example, a climbing club, a choir, a debating group.
- lead to more agencies who support children, working more effectively together. For

example, a nurse would be able to collaborate with a learning mentor*.

- offer a lot more involvement to parents than a non-extended school. For example, a parent might come on site and do a yoga class and take the opportunity to look at their child's work on display.

Further Information
Open Evening/Visit
The school might have an extended services' manager. It is worth finding out. If not, ask a teacher about the member of staff responsible for extended services. It is a good sign if the person responsible for extended services is high profile and well known by other staff.

Prospectus
This should include information about the school's extended services. It should say how 'extended' a school is, whether for example, it is a full extended school.

School Publications
The school newsletter should include information about the extended services taking place. You can contact the school and ask to be sent the latest edition. The website should give you an indication of what extended services are currently available.

To sum up:
At the time of writing, schools will be 'extended' to differing degrees. It is worth finding out what extended services they offer and whether they might benefit your child.

Faith Schools

Around 600 secondary schools are faith schools*
and the overwhelming majority of these are
Christian. Many of the new academy schools have
Christian sponsors.

- Faith schools have separate admissions criteria
  to other schools in the local authority. It is
  important to research these if you want your
  child to go to a faith secondary school.
- It might be that you are interested in faith
  schools because of the way religion is taught.
  Voluntary-aided* faith schools concentrate
  upon their own faith. Voluntary-controlled* or
  foundation* schools teach a religious education syllabus with a more multi-faith approach.
- There is a common perception that faith
  schools have a strong work ethos and char-
  acter. This is certainly the case in some faith
  schools, but it should not necessarily be taken
  as the norm. You need to view faith schools
  with the same critical eye as non-faith schools.

Further Information
Website
Different denominations and faiths have their own
websites detailing school provision. For example:
www.cesew.org.uk
The Catholic Education Service
www.cofe.anglican.org
The Church of England website

To sum up:
Research faith schools with the same rigour as you would non-faith schools.

Feeder Schools

A secondary school's feeder schools* are the primary schools from which it receives students. A secondary school's size, location and catchment* determines which feeder and how many feeder schools it has. Some secondary schools have three or four feeders, others forty or more.

- Schools which have a large variety of feeder primary schools can be a good choice if you want your child to have a sense of a fresh start and meet new people.
- Schools with only a few feeder schools can give your child a sense of continuity and security, if they attended one of the feeders.
- If a child joins a secondary from one of its main feeder schools, it is likely the secondary school will have knowledge of their primary school. This can aid the smoothness of transition*.

Further Information
Open Evening
A senior manager will be able to tell you the number of feeder schools the secondary school has, and what the main feeders are.
Primary School
Your child's current primary school can tell you what secondary schools it feeds into.

To sum up:
Whether your child is at a secondary school's feeder primary school or not can affect the nature of their transition to secondary school.

Grammar Schools

Grammar schools* are selective schools. They have an entrance test, often still called the 11 plus exam, which selects the most academic students. There are relatively few of them across the country.

- Most counties or boroughs do not have grammar schools.
- Grammar schools are usually hugely oversubscribed*, and therefore can choose not simply those students who pass their selective test, but those who do best in it.
- If your child is highly academic, likely to be successful in the test and to thrive in an intellectually challenging environment, then it is worth considering a grammar school.
- Unsurprisingly, grammar schools have a very good success rate of students going on to university, especially Oxbridge.

Further Information
LEA
Your LEA or neighbouring LEA Admissions sections will be able to tell you about grammar schools in your area.
Website
ngsa.org.uk

The National Grammar School Association

To sum up:
A highly academic student would be likely to thrive in a grammar school.

Local Education Authorities (LEAs)

The LEA* is responsible for delivering education for the council in a borough or county. It might be that you are in the catchment* area for more than one education authority. Or it may be you are considering moving to a particular LEA area to access different schools. It is therefore worth investigating the quality of provision on offer from different authorities.

- Authorities have reputations like schools do, and like schools they are often out of date. Do not automatically dismiss an education authority just because you have heard bad things about it.
- Some authorities achieve higher value added* results than others.
- Some authorities have the majority of their secondary schools achieving higher than the national average in exams, and some, the majority of schools below. It is important, however, to look at how individual schools' performance impacts on borough wide percentages. For example it might be that a few schools are carrying the results, while the majority of schools are underperforming. A good sign is if there is a consistency of

improvement or achievement. This shows that there is some overarching authority strategy that is working effectively.

- Authorities spend different amounts of money on schools. Sometimes this is as a result of government financial allocations dependent on local levels of social deprivation. Therefore, it does not necessarily follow that in an affluent area more is spent on schools than in an area of poor housing. Do not assume that if an area appears deprived, the schools are.

- Some authorities are more popular with teachers than others. This might be because of their reputation for teacher training or innovation. Therefore, some authorities may have a better field of teachers to choose from when appointing staff than others.

- It is worth pointing out that some authorities offer financial incentives to teachers for working in them. For example, it can be easier to recruit teachers in inner London because the additional salary allowance is greater than for outer London boroughs.

- Sometimes authorities that are less popular with parents are more popular with teachers. In these instances, parents might be missing out. It is therefore worth finding out from teachers which areas are popular to work in.

- Some authorities are always ahead of the game when it comes to new initiatives in schools while others fall behind. If you send your child to a forward thinking authority it is likely to be to their advantage.

Further Information
Achievement and Assessment Tables
Search the tables on the DfES* website by LEA. Look for consistency of achievement and see if your LEA's table compares favourably with its neighbours.
National Media – TES
Get an idea of what innovation is going on in different LEAs.
www.tes.co.uk
The TES* website
Ofsted
Education provision is assessed every year in each LEA through the Annual Performance Assessment (APA). In the Assessment's final judgements, the education services are given a grade, four is very good, three is good, two is adequate, one is inadequate. You can find each authority's APA on the Ofsted* website.
Open Evening
Talk to staff about what opinion teachers have of the local education authority.
Website
The LEA's website, under the designation 'schools', can give you some idea of what kind of provision to expect. If the web page is accessible, lively and up to date, then this is a good sign.
www.thenameofyourlocalauthority.gov.uk
The address of your LEA website

To sum up:
All LEAs do not offer the same quality of educational provision, and LEA reputations can be inaccurate.

Middle/High Schools

Middle schools* take students from Years 5 to 8, age 9 to 13. Most local education authorities in England do not have middle schools. They have a junior and secondary school system with students starting secondary school in Year 7.

However, a minority of local education authorities have a system where all students go from a primary or first* school, to a middle school to a high school.

- Middle schools are usually smaller than secondary schools, and so can be more accessible and less alienating.
- Middle schools give students access to specialist teachers and facilities, for example, Science teachers in Science laboratories, earlier than the secondary school system does.
- However, middle schools usually have fewer specialist staff and facilities than secondary schools, so in Years 7 and 8 your child could miss out on specialist subject teaching, such as Drama.
- A middle school system might give a student a disjointed experience, because they are educated at more schools than in the primary/ secondary system.

Further Information
LEA
You can find out from your own and neighbouring LEAs whether there are middle schools close to you.

To sum up:
A middle school might be more friendly and accessible than a secondary school, but it is likely to have fewer specialist resources.

Neighbouring Schools

When deciding upon the school for your child, it is important to investigate its neighbours, as they can impact on its status and success.

- A grammar school in an area where most schools are comprehensive, will have an effect on the intake of all neighbouring schools, even those in a different LEA. It is inevitable that the grammar school will cream off many higher ability students, which will leave neighbouring schools without the 'top' ten percent of students by academic ability in their cohorts.
- Popular single sex schools can affect the intake of their neighbouring mixed schools by leaving them with a gender imbalance.
- The intake of an undersubscribed* school will be affected by an oversubscribed* school in the same area. Some students will attend the undersubscribed school only until they can move to a vacancy at the oversubscribed school. Their move may have a negative effect on the value added score of the undersubscribed school.
- If there are schools which can select, for example academies, faith, or specialist in an area, then neighbouring schools may lose

students as a result.
- If there is an academy or a brand new school in the area, then this can have an effect on neighbouring schools. A school that was once oversubscribed can become undersubscribed because of demand for places at a brand new school nearby, or because of the high promotion of an academy.
- It is important to bear in mind then that the GCSE* results and value added score of a school are likely to be affected by its neighbours.

Further Information
LEA
When choosing the right school for your child, research its neighbours too. They can give you key information about your preferred school.
Open Evening
If a school you are interested in is in the same locality as a single sex school, ask them about gender ratios in their classes.

Case Study
In one borough there were 18 comprehensives. In the neighbouring borough was a girls' grammar school which was hugely oversubscribed. It had its own entrance exam and took the top ten percent of those who passed. School L, in the borough with 18 comprehensives, was oversubscribed. However, even this school was affected by the proximity of the grammar. In Year 7, two very bright girls had chosen to come to School L. However, they were on the waiting list for the grammar school. They

became part of School L's statistics in Year 7. The two girls made a very good start at the school and were happy. But when places came up at the grammar school they left immediately. Just the departure of these two students had a negative effect on School L's achievement figures.

To sum up:
A school's success is in part dependent on its neighbours. Sometimes successful schools work to the detriment of their neighbours, particularly their performance in Achievement and Assessment Tables*.

Single Sex/Mixed Schools

There is much evidence citing the benefits of single sex schools, so the choice of mixed or single sex is worth investigating:

- Some studies have shown[1] that girls can get better results if they are educated in a single sex environment.
- Girls' schools are often more popular with parents as a single sex option than boys' schools. It is often the case therefore that girls' schools in an area have a better reputation than boys' schools.

---

[1] Solidis, T. (2006) 'Literacy & Classroom Issues in Single/Mixed Sex Schooling', *Gender & Education*, Vol 18, no 2.

- Some parents send their children to mixed schools partly because they want to educate them in socialising with the opposite sex.
- Some argue that mixed schools have a healthier dynamic in the classroom than single sex schools. For example, a mixed classroom can bring to a subject a greater variety of learning styles and opinions than a single sex equivalent.
- Some parents send their child to single sex schools because they do not want them to be distracted by the opposite sex. In my experience, because they have reduced access to them, students in single sex schools can often become more fixated with the opposite sex.
- Single sex schools usually attract more teachers of the same sex as the students.
- Some schools which are officially mixed often end up with more of one gender than the other. This often happens if there is a preponderance of girls' or boys' schools among their neighbours. This is potentially *a cause for concern* and needs investigating. For example, a school might not necessarily be right for your daughter if in Year 7 most classes have 75% boys.

Further Information
Open Evening/Visit
Ask about gender ratios in the school. Ask the student showing you round about the distractions or otherwise of the opposite sex at their school.

To sum up:
The decision of mixed or single sex is largely down to what you feel would most suit your child.

6th Form

A 6th form* might not seem a priority when considering a school for your ten year old. However, if schools have 6th forms in your area taking them into account is useful when making your decision.

Post 16 provision varies between LEAs, from 6th Forms in all schools, to few or no school 6th forms and reliance on FE* colleges.

- A good 6th form can give younger students something to aim for. 6th formers often have special dispensations, like the chance to wear their own choice of clothes rather than uniforms, to which other students aspire.
- If the 6th formers are good role models, then they can be a civilising influence, and can often be used as mentors to younger students.
- Some teachers prefer working in schools with 6th forms. 6th form teaching is often seen as a bonus and an intellectual challenge. Therefore, schools with 6th forms can sometimes have a better field of applicants for jobs than schools without.
- Continuity of teaching staff can positively influence levels of achievement amongst young people. Students who want to continue their studies in the 6th form can benefit from working with teachers who are already familiar

with their learning styles and potential from the lower school.

- A school with a good 6th form often attracts 6th form students from other schools. This can give the school a new energy and a greater degree of diversity.

- In LEAs where 6th forms are rare, the few schools that do have them may have a more academic atmosphere than their neighbours.

- An ineffective 6th form can affect the whole school. The older students might be poor role models and demonstrate an attitude of indifference to learning. Disappointing results in the 6th form can set low standards for the rest of the school.

- If schools with a 6th form have a low staying on rate, then this is *a cause for concern*. It is likely that its students do not have faith in its post 16 courses. If the school has 100% staying on rate into the 6th form then this can also provoke questions. Schools are well paid per pupil in the 6th form and an artificially high figure might suggest that a school is persuading students to stay on for the wrong reasons.

- If your child is a late developer, then it might be appropriate to send them to a school without a 6th form. If they gain a reputation for under achievement in the lower school then this will follow them to the 6th form. They might stand a better chance of achieving highly after the age of 16 at a Further Education college, which would have fresh expectations of them.

Further Information

Prospectus

The school brochure should give you information about the 6th form and its results. Look for what the 'A' Level* and vocational course* results have been for the last three years. Trends should be upwards. If there are subjects which have high levels of failures then that is *a cause for concern*.

Ofsted

The Ofsted report has a separate section on the 6th form.

Open Evening/Visit

Make sure you ask to see the 6th form at work, or at least speak to a 6th former. You need to make a judgement about what kind of role models the 6th formers provide. Make sure you talk to lower school students about the 6th formers. Find out whether students aspire to be in the 6th form and why. Find out what the staying on rate into the 6th form is. If it is 100% or below 25%, be suspicious.

School Profile

The profile has a separate section on the 6th form.

Case Study

G School claimed that it had a 100% staying on rate into its 6th form, to give the impression that it had inspired all its students to take on board the benefits of lifelong learning. It was not lying about the statistic, but staying on for some young people certainly benefited the school more than it did the students.

The 6th form was good at maintaining high academic standards, and had stringent entry requirements for all students who wanted to take 'A'

Levels. However, because it wanted 100% uptake, it had practically no entry requirements for vocational courses. Many vocational students were on inappropriate courses and would have fared much better at a Further Education college.

To sum up:
The nature of a school is affected by whether it has a 6th form, and the effectiveness of a 6th form impacts on the whole school.

Size of School

Secondary schools are usually between four and twelve form entry, taking in from 120 to 360 students in Year 7*. This range offers a variety of experiences for the secondary student.

- Some students who have been at a small primary school, for example, one form entry, and who might find the transition* to a large secondary school difficult, may flourish best in a smaller secondary school.
- In a smaller school it is easier for the staff and students to get to know each other as part of the community. In a school of 600 students, a good Head teacher will know the names of most of children.
- If your child has had problems at primary school, sometimes anonymity can be a benefit. In a small school, if a student misbehaves, everybody knows about it. In a larger school, it is easier to start with a clean sheet.

- Smaller schools are often forced to have closer links with their community and other schools because they are not big enough to function in isolation. This can enrich the curriculum for students.
- Sometimes, by Year 6, students feel restricted by the size of their primary school and a large secondary school can be a liberation for them.
- A large school can be alienating. For example, when I worked in a school of 2300 students, after three years, I was still coming across children I had never met before.
- Larger secondary schools can often afford to have more resources on site than smaller schools, for example a drama studio or well resourced gym, from which your child might reap benefits.
- Larger schools sometimes offer a more diverse curriculum because they have more staff available with a greater variety of specialisms, and more students to make classes viable.
- Often, large schools create smaller groups within them through House* systems. If these are successful, a student can have the best of both worlds, the facilities of a larger school with the intimacy of a smaller one.

Further Information
Ofsted
The front page of the Ofsted report gives you the number of students on roll.
Prospectus
This will usually tell you how many students are on roll and what form entry the school is.

School Profile
The front page of the profile gives you the number of students on roll.

To sum up:
Both small and large schools have benefits. The choice depends on your child's disposition and previous educational experiences.

Specialist Schools
Also known as 'Specialist Colleges'

Specialist schools* focus on a particular subject or group of subjects as their area of excellence. Currently 80% of secondary state schools in England are specialist. The government intends to increase this percentage to all but 200 schools by 2008. All schools have to apply to become specialist, except for academy schools which can become specialist schools automatically.

Specialist schools are called colleges; a specialist school's title might be 'G School, an Arts and Media College.'

Schools can specialise in teaching the Arts, Business and Enterprise, Engineering, the Humanities, Languages, Mathematics and Computing, Music, Science, Sports, vocational subjects or Technology. The most popular specialism that schools apply for is Technology. Successful specialist schools can have more than one specialism.

Specialist schools have a particular focus on those subjects relating to their chosen specialism but must also meet National Curriculum* requirements and deliver a broad and balanced education to all students.

Specialist schools can select 10% of their students according to their aptitude in the specialist areas, although the majority do not exercise this option.

- Specialist schools receive an additional government grant which means they usually have more money to spend on students than non-specialist schools.
- Overall achievement in exams and value added is generally higher in specialist schools than non-specialist schools.
- Specialist schools should have exemplary teaching in their specialist area(s).
- They are often popular with teachers whose subject is their specialism.
- Specialist schools usually have better resources in their specialist area(s) than non-specialist neighbours. For example, expect to see excellent ICT* provision in a Technology College.
- Specialist schools are required to have good links with neighbouring schools through their specialism(s). Therefore, specialist schools might help make transition easier between primary and secondary school.
- Often specialist schools have good links with the local community, voluntary organisations, and local businesses through their specialism. This can enrich the curriculum and sometimes help to make students more outward looking.
- Specialist schools often provide a greater

variety of qualifications in their specialism than is available normally. This gives their students a better chance to pursue the specialist subject in different ways. For example, in an Arts and Media college, a student might follow an academic course in Media or a vocational course in Media Editing.

- If your child already has a subject preference, for example, enjoys Art far more than Science, it is worth investigating schools which have that specialism.

- In reality, some specialisms make little difference in a school. Schools have to re-apply for their specialism every four years, which usually keeps them focused. However, it might be that when they first applied for specialist status they had strong teachers in one department who have now gone. Or it might be that they had students who were performing particularly well in one subject, who have now departed. As a parent then, it is important to check whether the specialism is established in practice or merely tokenistic.

- If a specialist Arts College puts on a poor play or has weak student Art work on display, then this is *a cause for concern*. If a specialist Sports College has a lot of supply* staff in their PE department then this is *a cause for concern*.

Further Information
Achievement and Assessment Tables
The subjects within the specialism should out perform other subjects, or at least do well by comparison.

Extra-curricular

If you are considering a school with a specialism that relies heavily on extra-curricular events, for example, plays or concerts, contact the school, ask when the next performance is, and attend.

Ofsted

The Ofsted report will comment on how well a school is developing its specialism.

Open Evening/Visit

The school's resources in the specialism should be first class. The work on display for that specialism should be of an exceptionally high quality.

School Publications

If the school is a Technology College, then all school publications, for example, newsletters, websites and prospectus, should be of an excellent standard.

To sum up:

It is a good idea to match any subject preference your child might have with a school specialising in that area. However, you must investigate whether the specialism is established or tokenistic.

Chapter 2 – The Basics

Achievement and Assessment Tables

Also known as 'League Tables', or 'Performance Tables'

Where to Find Them

www.dfes.gov.uk

The government publishes national league tables of school performance. These show how well students at each school have done in their exams at ages 11, 14, 16 and 18. The tables that tell you about achievement at age 14 are the Key Stage 3* tables. They are published in March for the previous academic year. The tables that tell you about achievement at age 16 are the Key Stage 4* tables, GCSE* or equivalent. They are published in January for the previous academic year.

The best place to find the tables is on the DfES* website, but they are published in most national and local newspapers when the data is released.

The tables include all schools in England, state* and independent*. Schools are listed alphabetically for each LEA*, with special* schools shown separately at the end of each list. However, the DfES website allows you to search for schools individually, giving you a comprehensive report on each school.

League tables can provide useful information to help choose the right school for your child. For example, you can compare how well all the schools that you may be interested in, have done.

However, it is useful to know how to interpret the information correctly, be familiar with the tricks of the trade, and use the information in conjunction with other key resources, if you are going to get an accurate picture of a school.

Which Table to Look at

The tables which give you the most useful information about which secondary school is right for your child are the Key Stage 4 tables. There are many reasons for this.

- At Key Stage 3, students only take exams in English, Maths and Science, so you do not get a full picture of achievement across the school.
- Schools normally take GCSEs or equivalents more seriously than Key Stage 3 exams.
- Students and parents do not usually take Key Stage 3 exams as seriously as they do GCSEs or equivalents, because it is the GCSE exams that they need to get jobs or college places.
- Historically, there have been inconsistencies in the marking of Key Stage 3 exams, and their accuracy is generally less trusted than that of

GCSE results.
- Key Stage 5* results are not such a clear indicator of the school's overall achievement as Key Stage 4 because students usually choose the subjects they are most successful in to study at Key Stage 5. Also, the school intake has often changed; new students will have arrived, some students from the lower school will have left.

This section is therefore going to focus on the Key Stage 4 tables.

Key Stage 4 Achievement and Assessment Tables

These tables give information on 15 and 16 year olds at the end of Year 11, who have just completed their GCSEs or equivalent. There is a lot of information here, so it is important to identify the most useful aspects.

The key statistics are:

Level 2

The most often quoted statistic is the percentage of students achieving five or more grades, A*–C at GCSE or equivalent. This measure is called Level 2 in the tables.

It is important to note that from 2006, alongside the Level 2 statistic, will be the percentage of students achieving five or more grades, A*–C, including English and Maths GCSE and from 2007 this will replace the Level 2 statistic.

Level 1

This statistic is the percentage of students achieving five or more grades A*–G at GCSE or equivalent. G is the lowest GCSE grade.

It is important to note that from 2006, alongside the Level 1 statistic, will be the percentage of students achieving five or more grades, A*–G, including English and Maths GCSE and from 2007 this will replace the Level 1 statistic.

SEN

This is the percentage of students with Special Educational Needs* who took GCSEs or equivalent with and without statements*.

Key Stage 2 to Key Stage 4 Value Added

This tells you how much progress students have made from age 11 to age 16.

Key Stage 3 to Key Stage 4 Value Added

This tells you how much progress students have made from age 14 to age 16.

Both the above statistics are presented in the form of a number above or below a thousand. The higher the number is over 1000, the more value a school adds. If the number is below 1000, the school loses value for its students.

Year on year comparison of GCSE results over four years

This table compares schools' improvement over four years using the Level 2 percentage.

The best way to use the Key Stage 4 tables is to bring up on the DfES website all the schools in the LEA where you live, or the LEA in whose schools you are interested, and compare them with each other.

These key statistics are explained in more detail below.

Level 2

This is the percentage of students at a school who have achieved five or more grades A*–C at GCSE* or equivalent. The GCSE grade scale runs from A* to G. However, A*–C grades are commonly regarded as GCSE passes and a D grade is generally seen as a fail. 57% of pupils nationally achieved Level 2 in 2005.

Example of School and College Achievement and Assessment Tables GCSE and equivalent level 2:

	% of pupils achieving
	Level 2 (5 or more grades A*–C)
LA Average	49.3%
England Average	57.1%
School A	52%
School B	100%
School C	36%
School D	51%
School E	64%
School F	No pupils at KS 4
School G	18%
School H	64%

'Equivalent' means alternative qualifications, such as the vocational GNVQ* soon to be superseded by BTEC* which have equal status to GCSE. It is important to note that a GNVQ can count for up to four GCSEs.

From 2006, alongside the Level 2 statistic, will be the percentage of students achieving five or more grades A*–C including English and Maths GCSE and from 2007 this will replace the Level 2 statistic.

The Level 2 statistic tells you:

- how a school performs in comparison to the national average and its neighbouring schools.
- something about how able students are at the school regardless of value added*. Usually the more able the students, the higher the percentage of five or more A*–C.

Look at this statistic in conjunction with:

- Comparisons of a school's GCSE results over four years. The five or more A*–C percentage for one year only can be misleading. A single statistic may be a one-off due, for example, to a particularly able or less able cohort. It might be lower than the national average, but still the highest percentage the school has ever had, indicating school improvement. The percentage might be higher than the national average, but it might be the lowest result the school has had in a number of years. In this case, the school could be in a trend of decline.
- SEN*. The higher the percentage of SEN students, with or without statements*, the harder it is for a school to get a high five or more A*–C percentage. It is therefore important, if you are comparing schools, to compare the SEN percentage. If two schools have a very similar five or more A*–C percentage, but differing SEN percentages, the school with the higher SEN percentage has probably done a better job of raising achievement.
- Key Stage 2 to Key Stage 4 Value Added. A school might have a five or more A*–C grade percentage that is higher than the national average, but a low value added* score. This means that although their students achieved high grades, they did not reach their potential; they could have done better. It might be the case that the school did not challenge its students enough. If a school achieves a lower than average 5 A*–C percentage, but a high

value added score, it means that they have been successful at fulfilling their students' potential.

Issues with the statistic:

- The GNVQ 'trick'. Schools are now wise to the fact that the GNVQ qualification, to be superseded by BTEC, is potentially worth four GCSEs at A*–C. Therefore, a GNVQ pass for most pupils can skew the A*–C percentage considerably. Some schools have made it compulsory for all of their students to do a GNVQ in the same subject, most commonly ICT*. By focusing a lot of energy on this one subject and qualification, schools can easily inflate their percentage for five or more A*–C or equivalent grades. Some of the country's most successful state schools have based much of their improvement on this method. However, from September 2006, the GNVQ trick will have less effect when GCSE Maths and English must be taken into consideration. Then, those schools which have focused upon GNVQs to the detriment of the traditional GCSEs will appear to be in a less healthy position.
- This statistic tells you little without value added information. For example, a school might have a cohort of very bright students, the majority of whom achieve five or more A*–Cs. But they all could have underachieved. The majority of the students could have been awarded B grades, when they had the potential to attain A grades.

Level 1

Example of School and College Achievement and Assessment Tables GCSE and equivalent level 1:

	% of pupils achieving
	Level 1 (5 or more grades A*–G)
LA Average	89.1%
England Average	90.2%
School A	95%
School B	100%
School C	96%
School D	92%
School E	95%
School F	No pupils at KS 4
School G	91%
School H	97%

This statistic tells you:

- whether a school is serious about all of its students, not just the high achievers. This percentage should be in the high 90s. A school which takes all its students seriously and does its best for those of every ability should endeavour to make sure that all have A*–G grades. If this percentage is low, then the school may be just focusing on those students who are going to bolster the five or more A*–C percentage.

SEN

This section focuses on how many special educational needs* (SEN) students the school has and what this means to you. SEN students with statements* have more serious special educational needs than those without.

Example of School and College Achievement and Assessment Tables GCSE and equivalent SEN:

	SEN, with statements		SEN, without statements	
	Number	%	Number	%
LA Average		5.3%		22.7%
England Average		3.8%		12.2%
School A	2	1.7%	9	8.5%
School B	0	0.0%	8	2.0%
School C	4	2.8%	88	60.9%
School D	8	5.6%	24	16.7%
School E	1	0.5%	14	6.2%
School F	No pupils at Key Stage 4			
School G	0	0.0%	61	45.1%
School H	9	5.0%	7	3.7%

This statistic tells you:

- some context for the Level 2 data. The more SEN students a school has, the harder it is for the institution to achieve high GCSE or equivalent scores. If the school has a higher number of SEN students than the national average, then this should be taken into consideration. If a school has a percentage of SEN students much lower than the national average, then you should have high expectations of their five or more A*–C percentage.

Key Stage 2 to Key Stage 4 Value Added

This table shows how much progress students have made from Year 6 age 11, when they take their Key Stage 2* SATs* in primary school; to Year 11 age 15/16, when they take their GCSEs or equivalent at secondary school.

Example of School and College Achievement and Assessment Tables KS2 to KS4 Value Added:

| | KS2 to KS4 Value Added | | |
| | Measure centered on 1000 | Coverage | Number of qualifications |
	VA measure based on progress between KS2 and KS4	% of pupils at the end of KS4 included in VA calculation	Average number of qualifications taken by pupils in KS2–KS4 VA calculation
LA Average	999.6		
England Average			
School A	992.9	92%	9.8
School B	1012.7	98%	9.6
School C	1038.3	96%	9.3
School D	1025.2	93%	9.7
School E	989.9	85%	9.3
School F	987.1	96%	12.0
School G	993.6	96%	9.5

The first column is the important one. The higher the number is over 1000, the more value a school adds. If the number is below 1000, the school loses value for its students over the course of Years 7–11.

Key Stage 3 to Key Stage 4 Value Added

This table shows how much progress students have made at the school from Year 9 age 14, when they took their Key Stage 3 SATs; to Year 11 age 16, when they took their GCSEs.

Example of School and College Achievement and Assessment Tables KS3 to KS4 Value Added:

| | KS3 to KS4 Value Added | |
| | Measure centred on 1000 | Coverage |
	VA measure based on progress between KS3 and KS4	% of pupils at the end of KS4 included in VA calculation
LA Average	1006.4	
England Average		
School A	1009.2	93%
School B	1010.8	98%
School C	1014.6	96%
School D	1005.7	98%
School E	1016.4	94%
School F	1008.9	93%
School G	997.7	99%

The first column is the important one. The higher the number is over 1000, the more value a school adds. If the number is below 1000, the school loses value for its students.

These value added statistics tell you:

- how good the school is at fulfilling a child's academic potential. The more value it adds, the more potential it is squeezing out of its students. In this respect, it is a more reliable indication of a school's effectiveness, than the overall five or more A*–C percentage. The value added grade should be looked at in combination with the A*–C percentage.

- how good a school is at building on what has been achieved at primary school during Key Stage 2.
- how good a school is at building on its own successes at Key Stage 3 during Years 10 and 11.

Issues with the value added statistics:

- For the KS3 to KS4 statistic, it is important to note that if a school does comparatively badly at the end of Key Stage 3, then this will inflate the Key Stage 4 value added score.
- There are lots of factors beyond a school's control, which may hinder the adding of value. For example, a child might have a high prediction as a result of their Key Stage 2 tests. However, they could come from an unsettled background. They might live in a house with no books. They might come from a household where they can engage in little conversation. They could live in an area where teenage disaffection is common. If any of these cases apply, a school could be very effective at adding value, but the student might make little measurable progress because of all the uncontrollable outside variables. By contrast, a child might have an average prediction as a result of their Key Stage 2 SATs. However, they could come from a settled background, where homework and learning are encouraged. Their house

could be full of books. Over every evening meal, the family might have challenging conversations. They might live in an area where the prospect of youth disaffection is unlikely. They may have positive learning role models. In this case, the school would find it much easier to ensure that value was added for the child, as there are fewer obstacles in the way and much more positive assistance from home.

- When schools have a high turnover of students like is never measured with like. The statistics take no account of pupil mobility so they may be comparing two very different school populations over a five year period.

- Schools which take in a higher number of high achievers in Year 7 can find it easier than others to achieve a high value added score. This is in part because they are likely to have fewer students who become disaffected by Year 11 and underperform in their GCSEs or equivalent, or drop out completely.

- A school that is oversubscribed can limit its intake of disaffected students and can find it easier than other schools to achieve a high value added score. However, it could be the case that they have had to work less hard for it.

- Schools which take in a high number of students whose first language is not English, EAL* students, are likely to have a lower value added score. These students might make excellent progress, but because of their lack of English, they may underperform in the SATs and GCSE examinations which measure value added.

- Generally the more SEN students a school has, the harder it is for it to have a high value added score. This is because SEN students might make substantial progress, but they may find it more difficult to succeed in the formal tests that measure value added. Also, non SEN students might make excellent progress, but the overall value added score will be reduced by the achievement of those with SEN.

Year on year comparison of GCSE results over four years

This table shows the schools' year on year percentage of five or more A*–Cs or equivalent for the last 4 years compared to the LEA and national average.

Example of School and College Achievement and Assessment Tables GCSE and equivalent results over time:

	% of 15 year old pupils achieving 5+ A*–C (and equivalent)			
	2002	2003	2004	2005
LA Average	42.7%	44.9%	48.3%	49.6%
England Average	51.6%	52.9%	53.7%	56.3%
School A	32%	29%	43%	41%
School B	68%	68%	62%	64%
School C	59%	63%	57%	59%
School D	96%	95%	99%	99%
School E	21%	31%	39%	34%
School F	37%	40%	45%	50%
School G	49%	52%	54%	57%

This statistic tells you:

- if a school has improved year on year. A consistent upward trend is a good sign.
- if a school's results have declined year on year, it is likely that this downward trend will continue.
- if a school is on the decline because the percentages begin above the national average and end below it.
- if a school's achievement is generally the same year on year. This is satisfactory, but it might suggest a school which is coasting or struggling to bring about improvement.
- if a school has no clear strategy for improvement. If the school's percentages are erratic, showing upward and downward swings with no clear improvement or decline, then this is *a cause for concern.*
- if a school is typical of the area.
- if a school is improving faster than other schools, which are likely to be in similar circumstances.
- if a school is underperforming compared to schools in similar circumstances.
- if students at a school are generally of higher ability than the national average.
- if a school has the capacity for sustained improvement. If the school's percentages start off under the national average and end above the national average then this is a very good sign.
- if a school is on the up, although the students are not necessarily those who are going to

perform well against national comparisons. This is evident when percentages improve but are under the national average.

Case Study

In one LEA, there were two contrasting schools. School T had one of the highest value added scores in the area. Because it was popular, School T was able to take a large proportion of high achievers in Year 7. It had few students with English as an additional language, and a low proportion of special needs students. The majority of its permanent excludees and the majority of students who left before Year 11 were SEN or EAL students. It had a poor record of keeping these students for the whole of the five years between Years 7 and 11. Consequently, by the time it came to Year 11 most of the students who would have negatively skewed the value added score had left.

School U had one of the lowest overall value added scores in the LEA. It had a higher number of SEN and EAL students in Year 7. There were very few permanent excludees. Students who were most likely to leave before Year 11 were high achieving students, who were on the waiting list for School T. School U added value to a much greater degree than School T for its SEN and EAL students. Interestingly, if you compared School U's added value for its very highest achievers with School T's, School U did significantly better. However, the national tables do not measure these elements of value added, so their achievements were not reflected by the national data.

To sum up:

The data from the Achievement and Assessment Tables is helpful but does not give you the whole story. Tables should be used in conjunction with each other and with information from other sources to glean a full picture of a school.

	Number of pupils at the end of KS4	% of pupils at the end of KS4		SEN, with statements		SEN, without statements		% of pupils achieving		% of pupils achieving at least one qualification	Average total point score per pupil
		aged 14 or under	aged 15	Number	%	Number	%	Level 2 (5 or more grades A*-C)	Level 1 (5 or more grades A*-G)		
	Cohort Information							**Results of KS4 pupils**			
LA Average					5.3%		22.7%	49.3%	89.1%	92.8%	330.5
England Average					3.8%		12.2%	57.1%	90.2%	97.4%	355.2
School A	118	0%	100%	2	1.7%	9	8.5%	52%	95%	97%	355.5
School B	149	NA	NA	0	0.0%	8	2%	100%	100%	100%	500.0
School C	145	0%	97%	4	2.8%	88	60.9%	36%	96%	100%	294.9
School D	144	0%	100%	8	5.6%	24	16.7%	51%	92%	89%	390.4
School E	222	0%	100%	1	0.5%	14	6.2%	64%	95%	99%	407.9
School F	School had no pupils at the end of Key Stage 4										
School G	140	1%	94%	0	0.0%	61	45.1%	18%	91%	98%	265.9
School H	180	0%	100%	9	5.0%	7	3.7%	64%	97%	98%	413.6

Sample Achievement & Assessment Table – GCSE and Equivalent Results – by LEA

Easy Guide

Achievement & Assessment Tables – GCSE and Equivalent Results – by LEA

Achievement & Assessment Tables are the subject of the previous section. On the opposite page is a sample Achievement & Assessment Table of an LEA's GCSE results. The highlighted areas are explained over the following pages.

Interpreting the Table

	SEN, with statements		SEN, without statements	
	Number	%	Number	%
LA Average		5.3%		22.7%
England Average		3.8%		12.2%

This borough has a considerably higher than average level of SEN students, level 2 percentages are therefore likely to be below the national average.

	SEN, with statements		SEN, without statements	
	Number	%	Number	%
LA Average		5.3%		22.7%
England Average		3.8%		12.2%
School C	4	2.8%	88	60.9%

This is an unusually high percentage. You might want to contact the school and check that this statistic is accurate. If it is, this would suggest that the school is not truly comprehensive because of a disproportionately high number of SEN students.

	% of pupils achieving	
	Level 2 (5 or more grades A*–C)	Level 1 (5 or more grades A*–G)
LA Average	49.3%	89.1%
England Average	57.1%	90.2%

It is important to note that from 2006, alongside the Level 1 and 2 statistics, will be the percentage of students achieving five or more grades, A*–C, and A*–G, including English and Maths GCSE, and from 2007 this data replaces the Level 1 and 2 statistics.

% of pupils at the end of KS4	
aged 14 or under	aged 15

This column can show whether any students have been 'fast tracked' and completed Key Stage 4 early aged 14 or under. Students can take GCSEs at any age. In this borough this obviously has not happened.

| | % of pupils achieving | |
	Level 2 (5 or more grades A*–C)	Level 1 (5 or more grades A*–G)
LA Average	49.3%	89.1%
England Average	57.1%	90.2%
School A	52%	95%
School B	100%	100%
School C	36%	96%
School D	51%	92%

A school with 100% level 1s and 2s could be a private school which selects, or it could be a school that uses GNVQs to achieve five or more A*–Cs for most students, as one GNVQ can count for four GCSE C grades. This tactic will have less of an impact from 2006, when English and Maths GCSEs have to be taken into consideration as one of the five or more grades A*–C, and A*–G.

	% of pupils achieving at least one qualification
LA Average	92.8%
England Average	97.4%
School A	97%
School B	100%
School C	100%
School D	89%

100% for at least one qualification suggests that the school is very inclusive, and all abilities are catered for.

	% of pupils achieving	
	Level 2 (5 or more grades A*–C)	Level 1 (5 or more grades A*–G)
LA Average	49.3%	89.1%
England Average	57.1%	90.2%
School G	18%	91%

There is serious underachievement at this school. Despite a high number of students with SEN, 18% is worryingly low.

School E

Refer back to the Table and look across the statistics for this school. It clearly has students whose ability is above average. It has fewer SEN students than the national average. However, given the fact that it has high achieving students, you might expect an even higher level 2 percentage. It would be worth finding out how much value they actually add.

School F	School had no pupils at the end of Key Stage 4

It is probably the case that this is a new school, and has not yet had students go through to Year 11.

	Average total point score per pupil
LA Average	330.5
England Average	355.2
School C	294.9
School D	390.4
School E	407.9
School H	413.6

This suggests that most individual students here fulfil their potential in their GCSEs or equivalent. The school is not just being carried by their level 2 students. A lot of the remaining students clearly just missed level 2.

	% of pupils achieving at least one qualification
LA Average	92.8
England Average	97.4
School D	89

This suggests a drop out rate that needs investigating.

	SEN without Statements: Number	%	Level 2 (5 or more grades A*–C)
LA Average		22.7%	49.3%
England Average		12.2%	57.1%
School D	88	60.9%	36%

Considering the number of SEN students at the school, 36% is a good result.

	SEN with Statements: Number	%	Level 2 (5 or more grades A*–C)
LA Average		5.3%	49.3%
England Average		3.8%	57.1%
School A	2	1.7%	52%

Given the low number of SEN students, you might expect the level 2 percentage to be higher.

Evaluation of sample schools

- School G is a cause for concern, and unlikely to be right for your child.
- School C does well with the students it takes in.
- School C appears to be inclusive of all ability levels.
- School A has an intake of high ability students, but might be coasting.
- School D might have a problem with catering for students who are at risk of dropping out.
- High achievement is distributed among students of all ability levels at School H.

Ofsted Reports

Where to Get One

www.ofsted.gov.uk

Ofsted* is the organisation which inspects schools, and makes a decision on how effective they are. From September 2005, each school gets inspected roughly once every three years. Prior to September 2005, each school got inspected about every four years.

The inspection is carried out by a team of Her Majesty's Inspectors, HMIs, some of whom have been, or still are teachers, Deputy Head teachers, Head teachers or advisers. They have all received training in 'Ofsted' inspections, and many inspectors have carried out a large number of inspections all over the country so they have much experience to draw on.

The nature of Ofsted inspections changed in September 2005. Previously, the school was informed about eight weeks in advance of an inspection, and the inspection lasted a week. The inspection team consisted of at least one inspector for each curriculum area. Most teachers would be observed in the classroom at least once, if not twice, and a large number of interviews with staff would take place. Now, schools are told two days in advance of an inspection and the inspection is much shorter at two days. The school has to maintain an ongoing self evaluation document, and the inspection tests to see whether the document is accurate, and whether the school has capacity for improvement, by carrying out a much smaller number of focused observations and interviews.

Previously, it would take a couple of months for the report to be published. From September 2005, it takes about two weeks for the report to appear on the Ofsted website.

A school can be deemed to be

grade 1   outstanding
grade 2   good
grade 3   satisfactory
grade 4   inadequate

Therefore, in the text, you are looking for the words 'outstanding' and 'good'. You can accept a certain amount of 'satisfactory' but not 'inadequate'. If a school is 'inadequate' it can be put into 'special measures'* and given 'notice to improve.'

The school is given a grade for overall effectiveness. Then the report is divided into sections and the school is given an individual grade for each section, except for the 'What the school should do to improve further' section. At the end of the report is a grid of 'Inspection Judgements', and a letter to the school's students from the lead inspector.

If a school's overall grade is 'inadequate' and it has been put into 'special measures' it is doubtful whether currently it is the right school for your child. However, all other categories of judgement can be considered.

There are different views as to whether every Ofsted report is an accurate reflection of a school. However, in the context of this book, it would be rash to advise parents to send their child to a school with an 'inadequate' overall Ofsted judgement.

If you are not able to read through all of the report, the most important parts are 'Overall Effectiveness' and the grid of 'Inspection Judgements'. If you just want a summary of the report, the 'letter to students' provides this.

There are two judgements Ofsted can make, which mean you would probably disregard the school from your wish list; special measures and serious weaknesses.

Special Measures

If a school fails its Ofsted inspection it is put into special measures*. A 'special measures' school is one that is *"failing or likely to fail to give its students an acceptable standard of education"* (School Inspections' Act 1996). It will state clearly in the first sentence of the 'Overall Effectiveness' section if the school is going to be put into special measures. A school is given support to get out of special measures and heavily monitored by inspectors until it does so.

Serious Weaknesses

If a school causes the Ofsted inspectors serious concern it may be deemed to have 'serious weaknesses'*. Some schools with serious weaknesses have many of the characteristics of a school that requires special measures, but not to the same degree. Other schools may have serious weaknesses in only a few aspects of their provision. It will state clearly in the first sentence of the 'Overall

Effectiveness' section if the school has serious weaknesses.

The Report – Section by Section

This section lists words that you might look out for to guide your understanding of the report. Words with a tick √ above them should reassure you, words with a cross **X** should cause you concern. I have not included in these lists the words that accompany the grades 'outstanding', 'good', 'satisfactory', 'inadequate' but these are your clearest guides in the Ofsted report.

To make this section accessible, I would advise you to read it with an Ofsted report in front of you.

<u>Front page</u>

- Dates. It is important to ascertain when the report was carried out. If it is over two years' old, and it is nearly time for the school's next inspection, bear in mind that things might have changed, particularly if there is a different head in post.
- The number on roll will give you an idea of the school size.
- Description of School. This section will tell you whether the school is oversubscribed and what kind of students attend. It might include how many students have free school meals*. It will tell you what their economic situation is,

their ethnic backgrounds, how many of them have special educational needs* or other learning difficulties, what languages they speak and measure all these areas against national averages. If the school is a specialist* school, it will be recorded here.

Overall Effectiveness of the School

This is the most important paragraph. If you read nothing else, read this.

The first sentence of this paragraph will assess the school overall.

√	X
Effective	Unsatisfactory

Teaching and or learning will be mentioned.

√	X
Good or better	Unsatisfactory
Excellent features	Passivity
High expectations	Greater pace
Challenging	Inconsistency

As will the curriculum on offer.

√	X
Motivates	Inappropriate
Inspires	
Appropriate	
Access	
Excellent range	
Innovative	
Suits needs	

The quality of behaviour is described and whether students enjoy school or not.

√	X
(very) High standards	Negative effect
Behave excellently	Poor
Respond well	
Calm	
Managed effectively	
Happy	

Progress and achievement are described. If progress is recorded as being "very good", this does not necessarily mean that the school has high GCSE* results compared to the national picture. What it means is that the school is good at adding value*, and the students have a very good chance of reaching their potential.

√	X
Above expectations	Variations in standards
Targets met	Underachievement
Positive impact on standards	Standards are still low
	Underperforming significantly

This section will tell you whether the school is safe and caring, and what attitudes the students and staff have towards each other.

√	X
Secure	Lack confidence
Caring	Health and safety concerns
Safe	
Mutual respect	

The quality of the Head teacher and or leadership team will be summarised in one or two sentences, as part of overall leadership and management.

√	X
Clear vision	Inconsistent
Purposefully led	Insufficient emphasis

As a parent, you are looking for improvement since the last inspection and capacity for further improvement in future.

√	X
Good capacity to improve	Notice to improve
Capacity for further improvement	

This section also discusses progress in 'personal development,' which means how well students develop socially through their relationships at school. As a parent, you are looking for good progress in both personal and academic development.

√	X
Learners enjoy their work	
High regard	
It is very good value for money	
High expectations	

This section might comment on how students progress in specific subjects, particularly if a subject was mentioned as weak in the last inspection.

The report will tell you if there are any areas of weakness. For example, it could say, "good progress academically in all subjects with the exception of English." If an exception is made for one of the core* subjects, then you need to explore what the reasons for this are. If the subject is mentioned in the section, 'What the school should do to improve further', you should ask at open evening or visit whether the school has carried out any of the recommendations. If they have not, then this is *a cause for concern*. If more than one of the core subjects are an exception to good progress, then this is *a cause for concern*. If the subject which is an area of weakness is a favourite of your child then this might not be the right school. If the subject where there is an area of weakness is the school's specialism, for example, Science in a specialist Science College, then this is *a cause for concern*.

Grade

The grade for this section is the most important in the report. You would be unlikely to consider a school for your child if this section had lower than a grade 3. It would not make any difference if the grades for the other sections were higher.

If the grades for other sections worried you but the grade for this section was very high, then you should be reassured.

Effectiveness and Efficiency of the 6th Form

The 6th form may not be your first priority, but this section is worth a glance. If the 6th form is 'outstanding', 'very good' or 'good' then you can put your mind at rest. If the 6th form is 'satisfactory' only, and you are imagining your child might be a student who stays on in the school post 16, then this might be *a cause for concern*.

What the School should do to Improve further

This section will almost always be filled in. In virtually every school Ofsted will see room for improvement. However, the fewer points the better. It is a good sign if the bullet points present show that suggested improvements will be building on good work already carried out, for example, "make teaching <u>even more</u> sensitive to students' needs."

If behaviour is mentioned, then this could be *a cause for concern* as behaviour issues impact on all students.

It is *a cause for concern* if all three core subjects, English, Maths and Science are named as needing to improve.

√	X
Further improve	Improve teaching in core subjects
Continue its work to improve	Improve behaviour

Grade
No grade is given for this section.

Achievement and Standards

This section describes exam results. It often tells you what the standards of the children were before they entered the school, whether they were below or above the national average. Then it looks at the subsequent progress they have made and whether that is below or above the national average. A comment is often given on the achievement of different learners, for example, low attaining students, SEN students, gifted and talented* students, or students from an ethnic minority. It will sometimes tell you whether the school has met targets set for it by the local authority.

All the exam levels will be covered, Key Stage 3*, GCSE and other Key Stage 4* exams, 'A' Levels* and other Key Stage 5* exams if applicable. It is important that the students excel at all stages, but the key year group to look for is Year 11*. If achievement at the end of Year 11 is unsatisfactory, then this is *a cause for concern*.

It is important to find out whether results have improved year on year and whether students make good progress. This shows that the school is on a positive trajectory. How the results measure up to the national average is interesting, however, it is important to note that the school's results might have improved substantially and the students might have made excellent progress on the basis of their ability, and yet results could still be below the national average.

√	X
High	Inconsistent
Excellent	Room for improvement
Improved markedly	Poor
Targets exceeded	Well below average

If there are any weak subjects that do not have improving results and students progressing, then it will be noted here. If a core subject area is weak, then this is *a cause for concern*. You would have to be reassured through a visit or open evening that steps were being taken to rectify the situation. If there is one weak subject area that is your child's favourite then this might be *a cause for concern*. If there are more than two subject areas that are cited as not improving, then this is *a cause for concern*.

Grade

If you want to send your child to an academic school where achievement is consistently higher than the national average, then only grades 1 and 2 are acceptable here. If your priority is that the school is improving, then grade 3 would not necessarily be a cause for concern if the paragraph was generally positive, and the grade for 'Overall Effectiveness' was high.

<u>Personal Development and Well-being</u>

This section will reveal whether students enjoy coming to school, how they behave towards their peers and how they feel about the school and their learning.

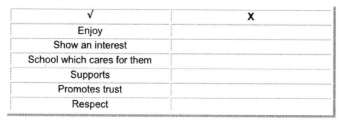

√	X
Enjoy	
Show an interest	
School which cares for them	
Supports	
Promotes trust	
Respect	

Pupil behaviour, attendance and punctuality are described here and attendance will sometimes be compared to the national average. If there are issues in one or more of these areas, then this is *a cause for concern*. School exclusions* will be commented on as will strategies the school adopts to cope with difficult students.

√	X
Very high	Unacceptable
Very pleasant	Disruption
Orderly	
Exemplary	
Fair	
Consistent	
Positive attitudes	

How students progress socially and emotionally is described through the terms 'spiritual, moral and social and cultural development'. Sometimes, this part of the report will comment on how types of students cope within the institution, such as those who lack confidence. You will find out whether Ofsted thinks bullying takes place, and whether the students feel safe. Here you can get an idea of the school's values, and how they educate their students in them. For example, is politeness something the students are taught to value? Or, is difference of opinion and diversity celebrated?

√	X
Safe	
Good relationships	
Confidence	
Enthusiastic	
Mature	
Sensitive	

In this section you can get an idea of how the school values the cultural heritage of its students and links to its wider local community. It will make it clear whether multi-culturalism is taken seriously and whether students have an understanding and tolerance of their peers. Any participation in the community will be commented on and sometimes attitudes of local residents to students will be included. If there is a student council, its effectiveness will be commented on here.

√	X
Celebrate their own culture	
Good participation in the community	
Effective contribution	

Health, physical well-being and the quality of school meals will be commented on. You will find out here how well students are prepared for their future and careers.

Grade
A high grade is important here if you want a school that educates the 'whole' child.

Quality of Provision

Teaching and Learning
This tells you what lessons are like in the school. The process of a typical lesson will be described in detail, whether it starts promptly, what the behaviour is like, and how teaching and learning take place. It will describe whether lessons are planned and well structured, beginning with clear and shared objectives, and involving appropriate and challenging tasks. How well teachers engage their students with a variety of techniques, and how well

students respond, will be commented on. Sometimes, the quality of teaching and learning for specific groups such as SEN or gifted and talented students is assessed. Here, Ofsted report on the effectiveness of marking and homework.

√	X
Promptly	Lack pace
Interested	Disruption
Range of techniques	Struggle
High expectations	Noisy
Independence	Slow
Take pride	Inconsistent
Excellent relationships	Little homework

Grade

This is another key area. This grade cannot be lower than a 3. If lessons are not well taught, then the school will find it very difficult to fulfil students' potential.

Curriculum and Other Activities

The report looks at what core and optional subjects are available for young people, examines whether there is a good range and whether the range matches the needs of the students. Both the curricular and extra-curricular provision on offer, and academic and vocational courses are described.

√	X
Broad and balanced	Does not meet their needs
Good range	Poor
Choice is wide	
Many other opportunities	
Rich variety	

Grade

Look for a high grade here if you feel your child is going to benefit from a strong extra-curricular offer or if you are looking for a wide range of subjects including vocational qualifications.

Care, Guidance and Support

The quality of the pastoral* system and students' personal development is commented on here. This section looks at the guidance the school gives students, for careers, options*, sex and relationships, drugs education, and how good the institution is at dealing with transition* between primary and secondary school.

√	X
Positive	
Friendly	

This section explains how well different groups, such as gifted and talented students and those with special educational needs are provided for. All categories of staff and their impact on students can be mentioned here such as learning assistants* and learning mentors*.

√	X
Good range of assessment information	Variable
Challenging targets	
Learners taking responsibility for their learning	
Very accurate	

The effectiveness of assessment methods and target setting are discussed. Marking is commented on, whether it takes place and whether it guides the students to improve.

Here you will find how hard the school works on its communications with parents and other outside agencies, and how it responds to emergencies related to health and safety and child protection*.

√	X
Good relationships	
Wide range of very good support	
Strong commitment	
Take pride in	
Safe	

Grade
This section is important if you value a supportive environment for your child. If your child has any special needs, for example, is gifted and talented or has learning difficulties, then you will be looking for a high grade in this section.

Leadership and Management

This section is in a large part a comment on the effectiveness of the Head teacher. If the Head teacher is weak, then the grade here will be low. It discusses how good the Head teacher is at leading her staff and students, whether she has a vision which is understood and shared by all stakeholders, whether she is good at communicating, and whether good team work is in place.

How well the school has been led since the last report is mentioned. If things were good in the last report, you want to see that they have remained good in this one. It is a positive sign if phrases suggest that the school is on an upward trend that will continue, for example, "Science specialist school status has already had a significant impact on the Science curriculum and is beginning to impact positively on the whole school." It is *a cause for concern* if a core subject has not improved since the last inspection, for example, "standards in English have slipped," but phrases such as "the school is working hard to remedy this" mean that you should not write the school off, but investigate further what their success in remedying the situation has been.

This section is also concerned with how good the school is at assessing its own progress and what structures are in place to ensure further improvement. It might comment on the stability of the staff and the effectiveness of their training. It is a good sign if a potentially promising future is referred to.

√	X
Rigorous	Insufficient
Clear vision for the future	Inaccurate
Well placed to continue improving	
Strong capacity to improve	

The Head's financial management skills will be examined, as will how effectively the school's resources and buildings are used and developed.

√	X
Value for money	Insufficient
Cost effective	

Additionally the role of the governing body will be commented on.

√	X
Challenge	
Holds the school to account	

Grade

If the grades elsewhere are very good, and the grade here is a little lower, then this is not a cause for concern, as it demonstrates that the school does well, in spite of leadership concerns. If other areas suggest that there is room for improvement, then the grade here must be a 2 or above, because there must be strong leadership to lead the improvement forward.

Text from Letter to Students explaining the Findings of the Inspection

This part of the report is interesting because it acts as a summary. Therefore, you can get a flavour of the report just by reading 'Overall Effectiveness' and this letter. The letter will always begin with something positive, so that gives you an idea of the school's most noteworthy strengths. For example, if standards of behaviour are highlighted at the beginning of the letter, then this is a good sign.

Lessons will be mentioned, and you will find out here if they are interesting, and whether students enjoy them and work hard.

In the latter half of the letter will be the inspectors' causes for concern. If teaching, learning or behaviour are mentioned, then you would certainly need to read the inspection in more detail.

Case Study
Jonathan's parents wanted him to get into School F which had a grade 2 'good' overall in a recent Ofsted report, largely because the school had a grade 1 for the section 'Standards reached by learners.' The grades students attained at GCSE were significantly above average.

He did not get a place at this school, but at School G which actually had a better Ofsted report, still with a grade 2 'good' overall, but with some 'outstanding' grade 1 features. Their grade for 'standards reached by learners' was 3, because the grades the students attained at GCSE were broadly average based upon their ability.

In his first year at School G, Jonathan was happy, not achieving to his potential, but his underperformance was not dramatic. His parents still wanted him to go to school F.

After only two terms, Jonathan got a place at school F, but he felt like a fish out of water. He found the pace too demanding, the expectations too high, and instead of trying to keep up, he gave up and his achievement rapidly declined. After a year, his parents sent him to a third school whose Ofsted report was an overall grade 3, but it was deemed to be on the up, it had just got a new Head teacher and had plenty of potential for improvement. Jonathan flourished at this school, because he was one of the highest achieving students. He very quickly got into their gifted and talented programme. The group of gifted and talented students was small, and Jonathan felt special, enjoying being a big fish in a small pond. In Year 11 Jonathan got ten GCSEs grades at A*–C, with four A* grades.

To sum up:
Different sections of the Ofsted report have varying significance depending on your priorities and the needs of your child. However, the grade for 'Overall Effectiveness' has to satisfy you. You would be very unlikely to be satisfied with a grade 4 under any circumstances.

Easy Guide

Ofsted Report: Grid of Inspection Judgements

Ofsted Reports are the subject of the previous section. Every report is summed up by a Grid of Inspection Judgements. Here is a sample grid with a commentary on key areas.

Key to judgements: grade 1 is outstanding, grade 2 good, grade 3 satisfactory, and grade 4 inadequate	School Overall	16-19
Overall effectiveness		
How effective, efficient and inclusive is the provision of education, integrated care and any extended services in meeting the needs of learners?	3	3
How well does the school work in partnership with others to promote learners' well-being?	2	2
Comment: **This grade is a cause for concern, rather than a consolation. What it shows is that even though partnership work is very good, it does not meet the needs of the students, otherwise the grade in the row above would be higher.**		
The quality and standards in foundation stage	NA	NA
The effectiveness of the school's self-evaluation	4	4
Comment: **This grade is a serious cause for concern. It suggests that the school is not a good judge of itself, and therefore is going to have trouble steering an accurate course for its future.**		
The capacity to make any necessary improvements	Yes	Yes
*Comment: **Must be a 'yes'***		
Effective steps have been taken to promote improvement since the last inspection	Yes	Yes
*Comment: **Must be a 'yes'***		

Achievement and standards

How well do learners achieve?	3	3
Comment: *This should be a 2 or a 1. You cannot afford for your chosen school to give your child only a satisfactory chance of achieving.*		
The standards[1] reached by learners	3	3
Comment: *This depends on how academic the school is you are looking for. But cannot be a 4.*		
How well learners make progress, taking account of any significant variations between groups of learners	3	3
How well learners with learning difficulties and disabilities make progress	3	
Comment: *You are looking for 2 or 1 if your child has learning difficulties and disabilities.*		

[1] Grade 1 - Exceptionally and consistently high; Grade 2 - Generally above average with none significantly below average; Grade 3 - Broadly average; Grade 4 - Exceptionally low.

Personal development and well-being

How good is the overall personal development and well-being of the learners?	2	2
The extent of learners' spiritual, moral, social and cultural development	2	
Comment: *The grade 2 in the two columns above shows a school that makes students feel happy and content, but as the 3s in 'Achievement and Standards' show, at the detriment of their academic success.*		
The behaviour of learners	3	
Comment: *You are looking for a 2 or a 1 here. If behaviour is only satisfactory, the bad behaviour of others will mean that your child might not get equal access to learning.*		
The attendance of learners	3	
How well learners enjoy their education	3	

Comment: **It is interesting that this is only a 3, considering the 2 awarded for 'personal development and well-being'. This shows that the school has a fundamental problem – students are happy at school but are not happy to learn.**		
The extent to which learners adopt safe practices	3	
Comment: **This grade should be a 2 or a 1. Safety should be better than satisfactory.**		
The extent to which learners adopt healthy lifestyles	3	
The extent to which learners make a positive contribution to the community	3	
Comment: **It is interesting that this is only a 3, considering the grade 2 awarded for 'partnership with others'. This suggests that the partnerships do not actually facilitate the students' access to the community.**		
How well learners develop workplace and other skills that will contribute to their future economic well-being	3	

The quality of provision

How effective are teaching and learning in meeting the full range of the learners' needs?	3	3
Comment: **If your child is SEN * or gifted or talented*, than this needs to be 2 or 1.**		
How well do the curriculum and other activities meet the range of needs and interests of learners?	4	4
Comment: **This grade adds to a picture of provision not matching need.**		
How well are learners cared for, guided and supported?	3	3

Leadership and management

How effective are leadership and management in raising achievement and supporting all learners?	3	3
How effectively leaders and managers at all levels set clear direction leading to improvement and promote high quality of care and education	3	
How effectively performance is monitored, evaluated and improved to meet challenging targets, through quality assurance and self-review	3	

*Comment: **The grade 3 for the three columns above shows that the leadership of the school is distinctly average. This would account for the lack of focus and mismatch of needs presenting in earlier sections.***		
How well equality of opportunity is promoted and discrimination tackled so that all learners achieve as well as they can	3	
How effectively and efficiently resources are deployed to achieve value for money	3	
The extent to which governors and other supervisory boards discharge their responsibilities	3	
The adequacy and suitability of staff to ensure that learners are protected	Yes	Yes
*Comment: **Must be a 'yes'.***		

The extent to which schools enable learners to be healthy

Learners are encouraged and enabled to eat and drink healthily	Yes
Learners are encouraged and enabled to take regular exercise	Yes
Learners are discouraged from smoking and substance abuse	Yes
Learners are educated about sexual health	Yes
*Comment: **All the above must be a 'yes'.***	

The extent to which providers ensure that learners stay safe

Procedures for safeguarding learners meet current government requirements	Yes
Risk assessment procedures and related staff training are in place	Yes
Action is taken to reduce anti-social behaviour, such as bullying and racism	Yes
Learners are taught about key risks and how to deal with them	Yes
*Comment: **All the above must be a 'yes'.***	

The extent to which learners make a positive contribution	
Learners are helped to develop stable, positive relationships	Yes
Learners, individually and collectively, participate in making decisions that affect them	Yes
Learners are encouraged to initiate, participate in and manage activities in school and the wider community	Yes
The extent to which schools enable learners to achieve economic well-being	
There is provision to promote learners' basic skills	Yes
Learners have opportunities to develop enterprise skills and work in teams	Yes
Careers education and guidance is provided to all learners in key stage 3 and 4 and the sixth form	Yes
Education for all learners aged 14-19 provides an understanding of employment and the economy	Yes
*Comment: **All the above must be a 'yes'.***	

Evaluation of Sample School

This would probably not be your first choice of school for your child because:

- this school is lacking direction as evidenced by 4 for 'self evaluation' and 'matching the curriculum with learners' needs.' The 3s in the leadership and management section show there is not the vision at the top to move the school forward.
- this school consequently short-changes its learners. They only have a satisfactory chance of achieving and being in a class that is well behaved.
- this school could be described as 'well meaning'. The 2s for 'well-being' and 'moral

development' show that the students are cared for and the school is interested in 'the whole child'. However, it would seem that this focus is at the detriment of achievement.

- this school does not give you enough peace of mind about your child's safety as 'The Extent to which learners adopt safe practices' is only a 3.

Open Evenings and School Visits

Open Evening

An open evening is an important event which can help you decide which school is right for your child. It can help with the answers to key questions:

- will your child be safe?
- will your child be happy?
- will your child be able to learn without distractions?
- is there a culture of learning at the school?
- is the teaching good?

Listen to the Head teacher's speech, question the teachers and students, take note of the displays and read between the lines of the demonstrations.

- It is important to remember that the school's open evening is a 'show'. It is not necessarily representative of what the school is like day to day. Some very successful schools put on very good shows. However, some schools that are desperate for clientele also pull all the stops out for this event. So, just because there are six different science experiments going on, violinists on the stairs, and *A Midsummer Night's Dream* in the drama hall do not assume that it is necessarily going to be the 'right' school.
- However, if a school makes no effort at all for open evening, then this is *a cause for concern*. It could be a sign of indifference, crisis or compla-

cency, all states that are not conducive to your child's success.

- Most open evenings consist of tours round the school, various performances, demonstrations, and speeches, usually from the Head teacher, and sometimes from the Head of Year* who will be responsible for Year 7. Often, students themselves are on hand to give the tours.

The Head Teacher's Speech

At most open evenings, there will be a Head teacher's speech. Undoubtedly, a Head teacher can make or break a secondary school; so it is worth paying attention.

- When the Head is speaking, try to decide whether you like and trust them, because if you choose their school, you are going to have to develop an effective working relationship which lasts for at least five years. If the Head is inspirational, that, of course, is a very good sign. If they inspire you, they are likely to inspire your child. It is a good sign if the Head talks about vision and direction in a way that makes you think they really have a sense of where the school is going.

The overall focus of the speech will give you some idea of what the Head's priorities are. For example:

- Do they emphasise the caring ethos of the school?

- Do they emphasise the academic record of the school?
- Do they focus on the high achievers, or on the achievement of all students?
- Do they talk as if they know the students and interact with them, or do they present as someone more detached?

It depends on what your priorities are for your child, as to which of these areas will be most important.

- It might be that you want to speak directly to the Head teacher before choosing the school for your child. If you decide to do this at the open evening, it is important that you ask a question that will tell you something about the Head. A lot of parents ask the Head teacher about bullying, because it is something about which they are concerned. However, the answer to this question will have been well rehearsed. A friend of mine, when choosing a school for his daughter, asked each Head, 'How long does it take to mend a broken window at this school?' He felt this was a good question because it took the Head teacher by surprise, so he received an answer that was unprepared. It told him whether it was important to the Head to take pride in his school and keep it well maintained. It told him whether the Head teacher was concerned with detail, and had a 'zero tolerance' attitude. It told him how quickly things got done in the school.

<u>Staff at the Open Evening</u>

Head of Year or House
The Head of Year or Heads of House will be present at the open evening. The quality of the person looking after a student in their first year of secondary education is crucial, particularly in a large school, where a child may have little contact with the staff member managing their progress. Often these staff members will give a presentation. If they don't, it is a good idea to ask to speak to them. It is important that you and your child have faith and trust in the Head of Year or House, and have your questions satisfactorily answered. It is important to find out the following from them:

- How do you ensure that Year 7 students settle into the school successfully? The Head of Year or House will be responsible for the well-being of your child in their first few weeks at the school so you need to be reassured that your child's welfare will be safe in their hands.
- What is your policy on bullying? The Head of Year or House will be the member of staff who addresses bullying issues in the first instance, and you need to feel reassured that they would sort out any problems effectively.
- How do you ensure children make academic progress in Year 7?

Head of Department
It is important to speak to Heads of Department*, particularly in the core subject areas of English, Maths and Science and find out the answers to the

following questions:

- Have your GCSE results gone up or down in the last few years? It is important to know whether they are an improving or declining department.
- How do you organise your classes, are they mixed ability* or setted*?
- What extra-curricular* provision do you offer? It is important to find out whether they are an enthusiastic department who go that extra distance for children.
- Parents should talk to the Head of Department for subjects that their child is particularly interested in, e.g. Music, and ask them the same questions as above.
- If there is a Head of Department not attending in a core or key subject area, then you need to ask where they are. If they are just absent for the night, there is little to worry about. Their second in department can answer questions. If they are on long term absence or if there is a vacancy in the post, you need to ask a senior member of staff whether the situation is going to be resolved by the time your child arrives at the school.
- In any school there will always be weaker subject areas, often because of staffing issues. It is rare that all three core subject areas are equally strong. You will usually have to settle for the fact that one might be 'good enough.' It is important, however, that you are satisfied with the core subject areas, as the qualifications they provide are the most marketable for

jobs, college and university places. If you feel that there are significant weaknesses in all three core areas, then this is *a cause for concern*.
- Similarly in non-core subjects, there will always be relatively weaker areas. What you must find out at open evening is whether areas where you think your child may flourish are strong.

Other Teaching Staff

It is a good idea to chat with other teachers who are present on the evening. There are key questions to ask them, which will give you much needed information about the school. For example:

- How long have you been at the school?

This will give you an idea of staff turnover. If they have not been there long, ask them to direct you to someone who has. If they cannot find someone who has spent more than 12–18 months in their department, then this is *a cause for concern*.

- What do you think of the Head?

Obviously, most staff will be professional. However, if they are particularly enthusiastic, then that is a good sign. If staff are inspired, loyal and happy, then they are likely to be committed to your child. If a member of staff is disloyal, it could simply indicate a difficulty between an individual and the Head teacher. Ask other staff; if you get a similarly disloyal response, then that is definitely *a cause for concern*.

- How does this school compare to others you have worked in?
- Would you send your own children to this school?

Teachers know schools. If they would consider sending their own children to the school, then this is the greatest recommendation you can get.

Teachers love to talk about their job. People are rarely interested! Having a chat with staff can give you a good insider's view of how schools compare.

Display

When you are touring the school, look out for up to date displays that celebrate learning.

- The standard of display should be consistent throughout the school. It is *a cause for concern* if there are areas where display is lacking. It should not take much for the school leadership to ensure consistency.
- Displays of students' work need to be up to date. It is not a problem if some framed art work is by students long gone. However, if the majority of the students' displayed written work is more than a term or two old, then this is *a cause for concern*. A good open evening should be showing off the school as it is, not as it has been.
- Display should be labelled with students' names and their year group. This shows attention to

detail, that individual children are valued, and that the display is for the students in the school, not just for open evening attendees.

- Display should be finished to a high standard.
- Displayed work generally should be accurate work. Sometimes work in progress is displayed, and in this case, mistakes are part of the process. But otherwise, work should be well presented and accurately spelt. If this is not the case, staff have not checked the work carefully enough and the school may not sufficiently value accuracy.
- In each department, students' exercise books should be on display. If they are not, ask for them. If they are not forthcoming, then this is *a cause for concern*. Again, check the dates of exercise books, they should be current. Exercise books should contain mistakes. A child does not learn if they do not make mistakes. What you should be looking for is that the books are well marked. That means that there should be ticks and corrections on every page. Every two or three pages, there should be a teacher comment. An example of good marking is when the teacher comments on the work so far, and sets a target for the next couple of weeks. There should be some marking scheme evident, such as numbers or letters. If there are only ticks, this is not good marking, and is *a cause for concern*. Do not be put off by spelling mistakes that have apparently been ignored as long as some have been corrected. It can be demotivating to pupils to correct every mistake.

- If a book is really well marked, you should be able to see progress taking place. This should be acknowledged by the teacher. For example, the student should be congratulated for having achieved a target that was set earlier on.
- A confident department will display a selection of books, not just those of the most able students. It is worth asking to see the books of pupils of all ability levels. Check to see if books have obviously been marked just for the purposes of the display. Be suspicious if pen colours don't match up, or if the comments have clearly been added later!
- All books should be marked, not just some.

Demonstrations

- It is a good sign if there are events and demonstrations given by a variety of departments. This shows a commitment to the school across the subject areas.
- All three core subject areas should have some kind of event or presentation. This shows they are confident and have a significant role in the school.
- It is an encouraging sign if the presentations are well polished. However, that is not necessarily everything. For example, a school could use the same few students at every public event. A good sign is the involvement of a range of students with clearly differing abilities, even if some demonstrations are a little rough round the edges.

- A specialist* school, however, should have a demonstration or presentation in their specialism of an impressive and professional nature.

Students

- There should be a significant student presence at the open evening. It is a good sign if students from a range of year groups and abilities are represented.
- You should expect the students to be presented immaculately, in full school uniform.
- The more responsibility the students are given, the better, because it shows that the school trusts them and fosters a culture of independence.
- Questions to ask students are covered in school visits.

School Visits

- It is vital to see the school in action, as well as attending the open evening. If the school offers tours during the school day, a pro-active parent should take them up on it. If it does not, ring and ask if you can be shown round. If the school is reluctant then this is *a cause for concern*.
- It is worth taking time off work and taking your child out of school for a visit to their prospective secondary. A child will have to attend school during the day, so it is essential that

they see what the school is like during that time.

- An alternative tactic is to telephone in advance and ask to be taken round at a time when official tours are not offered.
- No school can cover up what it is really like during its school day, even during a planned visit.
- It is important that on a planned school visit the Head teacher makes herself or her Deputy available. If this does not happen, then the school is not taking its future intake seriously enough, maybe because it is complacent, or maybe because it is disorganised.

- Things to look out for on your visit:

  - Are the majority of students 'on task' in most of the lessons that you see? If they are, your child will get a good opportunity to learn. 'On task' does not necessarily mean 'silent'. A school full of silent classes is not one that feels confident or creative enough to allow student interaction. 'Busy noise' is a desirable state.
  - How often do you hear teachers raise their voice? Very few schools are free of shouting. Arguably, sometimes, it is appropriate for teachers to raise their voice. But if there is constant shouting, then the school may not be calm enough for your child to learn effectively. The tone of calm authority from staff is something to listen out for.
  - Is there a particular subject that seems less

calm, or where students seem less focused? In this area, are there more teachers raising their voices? You need to find out if one subject area or more is weak in a school. It is *a cause for concern* if this area is English, Maths, or Science, or a subject that is important for your child.

- Do you see student misbehaviour going unchallenged? Students misbehave in all schools, no matter how good they are. But you should not be satisfied with misbehaviour that goes consistently unchallenged by staff, or unsuccessfully challenged. It is *a cause for concern* if you see misbehaviour out of lessons and teachers walking past as if it is not happening. In this instance, teachers are not taking ownership.

- How often do you hear or see students refusing to do what they are asked? Incidences of defiance are inevitable in all schools. However, if this type of behaviour is common, the school may have serious behaviour management issues which will hinder your child's progress.

- Are there senior staff about? For example, on your tour, do you see a senior member of staff telling a student off, or positively interacting with them? Senior staff need to have a presence. They are the ones who need to 'lay down the law'. They should also know the students. Visible, effective senior staff create clear boundaries within which your child can learn. You should not be satisfied if there are students misbehaving and a senior member of staff walks past and does nothing.

- How do students greet each other and adults? Are they polite? Are they respectful? The atmosphere needs to be civilised for your child to flourish in a safe working environment.
- Are you allowed into classrooms during lessons? If you are not the school might have something to hide. Make sure you get to see a variety of lessons.
- What are the corridors like when lessons are going on? If there are students wandering about, then there is an issue with the management of students, which is *a cause for concern*.
- Who shows you round? If a school uses students to show you round, it is a confident institution. However well students are primed, they will always give you the real picture. Make sure you get as much information out of the student guides as possible. Your child, after all, is potentially going to be in their position.
- What is the playground environment like? Try and get shown round over a break time or lesson change over. If a student is showing you round, you will soon find out whether there are any 'no-go' areas. However, it is important to note that groups of adolescents are often intimidating. When they are 'playing' things sometimes seem more out of control than they really are. Every secondary school playground can make adults who are

not used to schools nervous. What it is important to note is whether the students showing you around are intimidated? If not, you probably have nothing to worry about.

It is important to note that in most schools at lunchtimes, students are not managed only by teaching staff, but also by midday assistants*. Unfortunately, in most cases these staff are not as well treated and respected by the students as teachers. This is a problem I have seen in most schools and it is not specific to successful or unsuccessful schools.

– What are the toilets like? A level of graffiti is not unusual but is unacceptable. The students and caretaking staff really take pride in their school if there is no graffiti at all. Students always want good quality fittings and nice loo paper! So, if the toilets are in reasonable condition, it is likely that the students have a voice at the school, and they consequently take care of their environment.

• There are key questions to ask the students who show you round, in order to help learn whether a school is right for your child.

– What do you do if you get bullied at this school? The answer you want is 'tell a member of staff.'
– If you get bullied, what gets done about it? The answer you don't want is 'nothing'. The answer you want is 'it gets sorted out.'

- Are there any 'no go' areas in the school? You want to find out, for example, if there are areas where the smokers go, or that scare the younger students. You want to know if staff are vigilant, and maintain a feeling of safety throughout the buildings and play-grounds.
- How do older students behave towards the younger children? You want to find out whether there is the sense of a caring community.
- What are your favourite subjects? You want answers which reveal that students like lessons where they progress and are inter-ested in what they are learning. You want to find out whether there is a learning ethos in the school. You do not want to find out that students favour subjects because they 'get to muck about.' You want to find out whether there are key subject areas that are not successful in the eyes of the students. You do not want the answer, 'Oh, nobody likes Maths here, it's too hard.'
- Who is your favourite teacher? You want answers where the students like teachers who encourage them to learn. 'I like Mr G because he is fun, but we learn a lot too,' is good, but 'I like Mrs H because she is a laugh' is not.
- What do you want to do when you leave school? You want to find out whether there is an ethos of ambition backed up by knowl-edge. If they are intending to go to univer-sity, are many of their friends?

There are two other key areas to focus upon for the open evening and visit, and they have been given sections to themselves in chapter 3, 'The Detail' – Buildings and Environment and Facilities and Resources.

Case Study

School R put a lot of effort into their open evening. There were Science experiments with first class equipment, and a Drama production with expensive props. Exercise books in the English department were particularly impressive, and the Head teacher did a talk with state of the art power point technology.

However, although it was directed time*, only half the staff were committed enough to turn up. The English books on display were five years old, and were brought out every year, and the props were borrowed from the Head of Drama's am-dram society. Two Science rooms had been kept locked, because of graffiti scrawled in them on the day of the open evening. Only five percent of the students were actually represented either through display or attendance.

To sum up:

An open evening is a put on show – it is not necessarily how the school will be when your child goes there in the day. You must therefore combine attendance at the open evening with other avenues of investigation to get a realistic and rounded view of a school before you decide whether it is the right place for your child.

Easy Guide: Open Evening – Display

School visits and open evenings are the subject of the previous section. Here is a sample school display showing you what it is essential for a display to have, what is excellent practice, and what to look out for across the school.

Essential

- Work - well presented, on a good quality background, bordered if appropriate.
- If work is hand written, handwriting should be neat.
- Written work – relatively mistake free, unless work in progress.
- Clear title showing:
  - what the work is
  - what subject area
  - what year group
- All work should be clearly labelled with the student's full name.
- Titles and explanations should be typed.
- Work should be dated, and relatively recent.
- Work from exercise books, or work in progress, should be marked.

Excellent

- Across a department, consistency of presentation, e.g. all the titles should be in the same font.
- Explanation of the work in more detail. Should be mention of how it links to the National Curriculum.
- Display addresses pupils – shows it has not just been put on for the open evening.
- Work on display from students with a range of abilities, not just the highest ability students.

Across the school

- Variety of work, e.g. hand written work, typed work, diagrams, drawings, 3 dimensional display, photographs of students
- Somewhere, in every department's display, there should be evidence of Information Technology – for example, a piece work having been word processed.
- Consistency of display. All departments represented.
- Extra-curricular activities, e.g. school plays or school trips, should feature somewhere in displays.

The Prospectus

Where to Get One

Every school should have a prospectus. It can be obtained by phoning the school directly and they are usually given out at open evenings or visits.

The school has a legal obligation to include information in its prospectus regarding provision for the disabled, but otherwise prospectuses can vary a great deal. This section aims to help parents decipher what the prospectus is really telling them about a school.

First Impressions

- If you ask for a prospectus from a school and it is not sent to you, then this is *a cause for concern*. The office staff should be trained to take such requests seriously.
- A school prospectus should be consistent and clear. It should not have duplication, or contradictory information. The prospectus should be devised with a clear sense of parents as audience. It is *a cause for concern* if the prospectus doubles as a guide for Year 7 students, for example.
- The school and the prospectus should match each other. A good school is honest about the way it presents itself; it does not try and hide things. No school is going to include its serious weaknesses in the prospectus, nor should it.

However, it should be genuine about what the school has to celebrate, and play to strengths, not distort reality. A highly finished, organised, impressive prospectus is meaningless, if the school is low impact, disorganised and unimpressive. Therefore, the impression you receive from the prospectus should be the same as the one you glean from the school itself.

- Prospectuses vary from extremely high finish, glossy productions to photocopied black and white inserts in a folder. A glossy prospectus is not everything, but it does tell you that the school is concerned about its client group, and that is potentially a good sign. If a prospectus seems not to be trying very hard it suggests that complacency has set in, or that there is a lack of organisation and pride in the school. Whatever the finish, the document should reflect a culture of high expectations. A specialist Technology College should certainly have a high quality finished prospectus, otherwise its credentials are immediately undermined.

- It is *a cause for concern* if the prospectus describes school arrangements in vague terms, for example, 'occasionally', 'mainly', 'often'. The right school for your child must be clear about its systems. It is no good finding out that the Languages Department runs a trip to Paris 'often' if that means every four years. You need to know whether the trip runs annually for this information to be valid.

The Specifics

- The information and photographs a school prospectus features should be up to date. If they are not, this suggests a lack of care, disorganisation, and possibly a lack of transparency about the school's current condition.
- Photographs of smiling children suggest that learning is meant to be enjoyable in the school. Photographs of children doing different things, and not just sitting in class, implies that the school celebrates a diversity of teaching approaches. Any photographs of impressive resources, like banks of computers should be viewed with caution, and their existence confirmed at first hand on a visit. If a school is multi-cultural and values this, it will try and represent diversity in the photographs it chooses.
- The Head teacher will usually write a letter or an address to parents in the prospectus. This is the Head's chance to present her priorities, and key words and themes can give you a clue as to what kind of school she runs and whether her priorities match yours.

  - The Head might want to give a warm welcome in her address, emphasising that students are happy and the school is caring.
  - It might be important to you that the Head emphasises high standards in uniform, good manners, politeness and adherence to tradition.
  - A Head might want to make a point of

valuing lots of different skills that children may have, and give examples of what these might be, for example, 'gifted academically….good at sport….creative….'

- If a Head teacher thinks that the school's good discipline is a key to its success, then this is a place where she will mention it. However, of course this discipline must be seen at first hand on a school visit.
- If the Head teacher's address is difficult to follow, then this is *a cause for concern*. A Head teacher should be skilled in written communication.
- A Head teacher who invites you to come and visit, and spells out the process by which you can do this, shows an openness and confidence about her school.

- A prospectus will commonly contain sections on 'Ethos' and 'Values' which are supplemented or alternated with titles such as 'Aims', 'Entitlements', 'Vision'. As written headings and lists, these are good to see but tell you relatively little. They are only worth anything if you see them at first hand on your visit. No school is going to write, 'Values – We only genuinely value the bright children,' but this might be the case.
- There will usually be a section on current facilities and future plans. However, the facilities should be validated by what you see at first hand. Make sure you find out on your visit whether the plans are provisional or definite.
- It is a good sign if the prospectus includes a section on parents, as this shows that the

school values the parent/school partnership, and wants to collaborate with parents effectively. This section should outline the school's schedule and methods for contacting parents, for example, parents' evenings and reports. The prospectus should identify key people whom a parent would contact if they had a cause for concern.

Many schools have a 'home-school agreement' which requires a parental signature. This might be mentioned in the prospectus. However, whilst sometimes meaningful, often this is a paper exercise which has little impact on a child's career at the school.

- If there is a separate section on discipline, it should be precise and user friendly. If a school has reproduced a policy which is clearly for another audience, for example teachers, then the information is of limited use.

- The prospectus should tell you about what groupings a school uses for teaching students, whether they are taught in sets*, streams* or mixed ability groups*. If the school organises students into any kind of ability groups, then the prospectus should describe a transparent process for the composition of these groups. If the selection process seems vague, then this is *a cause for concern*.

- The prospectus should tell you if there are any specific teaching arrangements in different year groups; for example, some schools adopt a system in Year 7* which replicates the primary school day, and is supposed to ease the transition from primary to secondary school.

- The prospectus should tell you about the subjects students will follow at Key Stages 3 and 4*. The information should be laid out in such a way that you are clear what subjects are taught at each Key Stage. Even better, you should be given a clear sense of how much curriculum time is allocated to each subject area.

- After reading the prospectus, you should know if students have any choice over subjects studied at Key Stage 3 and how the options* process takes place before Key Stage 4 courses begin. You should know which subjects are obligatory, which are optional, what range of subjects there is to choose from, and when and how students get to choose them. You should know what vocational and academic subjects are on offer.

  It is *a cause for concern* if there appears to be no clear options process. Choices for students should not change radically year on year. This suggests a lack of focus and vision or a school without efficient organisational systems. Or it could suggest a high staff turnover which precludes long term curriculum planning.

- The prospectus should give you an idea of day to day life for your child at the school, either through a day's timetable, or a description of how students spend their time.

- The prospectus should tell you how tutor groups* and the pastoral* system are organised. It should make clear who is responsible for the pastoral system, for example, Heads of Year*.

- Schools should include information about extra-curricular opportunities for students. Study support should always be included in this list. It is a good sign if a school provides some kind of extended provision, like a break-fast club or after school homework club. If a school is successful in a particular after school sports' league, then this may be highlighted in the prospectus.

  It is a good sign if visits are celebrated in the prospectus. However, it is *a cause for concern* if trips are described which took place years ago, or that only happen occasionally. This suggests a lack of focus, resources or organisation.
- The prospectus should give you information about school meals and how the school addresses the issue of healthy eating.
- There will probably be a section on special educational needs – SEN*. If this section includes reference to the school's SEN policy, then you may want to verify it at first hand on a visit. What to look out for in the prospectus is an SEN section that acknowledges the variety of special educational needs there might be among the students, for example, social, emotional, and behavioural.
- The prospectus should have a section on gifted and talented*, or more able, students. It is *a cause for concern* if they are not mentioned, as there are high ability students in all cohorts who need an individualised programme with a high profile in the school.
- There should be a section on school uniform, or dress code. For a school where adherence to

the uniform is important, then this will be spelt out in the prospectus. However, any uniform policy must be seen working at first hand.

- The prospectus should mention homework, demonstrating that the school has a clear policy about what, when, and how much is set. It should explain why homework is valued, and how it impacts on school improvement. However, any description of the homework process should be checked out at an open evening or visit by looking at students' exercise books.

- Schools will usually present information on attendance, often for the last three years. It is a *cause for concern* for the DfES* if a school falls below 90% attendance. It is a healthy picture if the school has 93% or above attendance. The percentage of unauthorised absences, those not sanctioned by parents, should be below 1%. Schools should have systems to chase up absences, so that the only unauthorised absences are genuine truancy. Unauthorised absence which is above 1% is potentially a *cause for concern* and you should ask about this on your visit. You want to be reassured that truancy is not a major issue at the school. It is a good sign if attendance figures go up year on year. If figures have been below 90% in the past and they are above 90% for the current year, then the school is clearly working hard on improvement in this area. It is *a cause for concern* if attendance figures are decreasing year on year.

- The prospectus may include a section on how

Religious Education is taught in the school. A good prospectus may also mention spiritual and moral development. Unless this is a particular priority for you, this section is of particular interest only if the school has a religious nature.

- Prospectuses will normally include a statement on sex education. The provision of sex education in a school is a legal requirement, and the information should vary little between schools.
- The teaching of Citizenship* and/or Personal, Social and Health Education, PSHE* is compulsory and the information included should vary little.
- The prospectus should inform you about careers' guidance and work experience. An initiative called 'Work Related Learning' was introduced in 2004, and a school which has a strong vocational programme will seek to make something of it.
- A prospectus might include extracts from the school's most recent Ofsted* report. It is important to look up the report and not rely wholly on short quotes, as the school will be selective about what it includes.
- The prospectus will tell you whether or not the school has a 6th form*.
- A school will often include information on 'Post 16' or post 'A' Level destinations, outlining what the students go on to do once they have left.

    - It is a good sign if over 80% of the students have gone on to further education. This shows that the school has instilled a desire for lifelong learning.

- If destinations are spread over vocational and academic areas, this shows that the school gives students a clear picture of the choice on offer, and that it values diversity among its students.
- If destinations are mainly academic institutions, this gives a message about the school's ethos.
- If there are more than five percent of students unemployed, this is *a cause for concern*.

- A nice touch in a prospectus is:

  - The inclusion of a school newsletter. First of all, this shows that such a publication exists. Secondly, it gives you a flavour of the school's day to day life, and shows that the school feels confident enough to share this with you.
  - The inclusion of some direct input from students, for example quotes or artwork. This shows an effort on the part of the school to value and include the student voice.
  - The inclusion of named people to contact if you have queries about particular issues. This shows the school is serious about having genuine communication with you.
  - The inclusion of any letters the school may have recently received from the DfES or LEA* complimenting them on their improvement.

Logos and Mottos

The cover of the prospectus will often feature one or more logos. Some Head teachers are logo junkies, while others show little interest in them. Often, the organisations and awards the logos represent will have very little direct impact on your child. What logos often do is tell you what type of school it is, while others can give you an idea of particular areas of excellence. However, logos should match up with what you see in action at the school. If a school has, for example, a 'Sports Mark Gold Award', but their PE exam results are poor, and their sports' facilities leave a lot to be desired, then the logo is meaningless.

Examples of logos you might find:

Arts Mark
  – Arts Mark is awarded to schools which show a commitment to the full range of Arts: Music, Dance, Drama, Art and Design. Schools apply for the award, and there are three levels of attainment, 'Arts Mark', 'Arts Mark – Silver' and 'Arts Mark – Gold'.

Cisco Systems – Network Academy
  – 'Cisco Systems' is a company which provides an e-learning programme to students in networking and Information Technology.

Charter Mark
  – A school subscribes to be involved in the 'Charter Mark' process which ensures that organisations focus effectively on customer needs.

Excellence in Cities
- 'Excellence in Cities' is a targeted programme of support for schools in deprived urban areas. Schools involved in this project will have initiatives such as the 'aim higher'* programme, a 'gifted and talented' scheme, and learning mentors*.

Healthy Schools
- A school has gone through a process where they have met criteria relating to personal, social and health education, for example, how PE is taught, how health issues are dealt with, how healthy eating is given a high profile. 'Healthy Schools' is a DfES initiative.

Investors In People
- A standard granted to private businesses and public sector organisations which have committed themselves to the learning and professional development of their staff.

ICT Test Bed
- The ICT* Test Bed project gives schools access to high levels of ICT hardware and software and also provides the support required to maximise effective use. It is run by a government agency 'BECTA', the 'British Educational Communications and Technology Agency'.

National Mentoring Network
- An association of mentoring projects which offers support to members and promotes the benefits of the many types of mentoring schemes to schools and businesses.

School Achievement Award
- These awards were last made in 2003, so it is important to check the award date. They were given to schools which had either made significant rapid improvement in results, or had made improvement that was significantly higher than in schools with similar circumstances, for example, a similar intake. These awards were a DfES intitiative.

Specialist Schools
- Each specialism has its own logo. A specialist school is often referred to as a college. Schools can be specialist in Arts, Business and Enterprise, Engineering, Humanities, Languages, Mathematics and Computing, Music, Science, Sports, and Technology.

Sport England
- 'Sport England' is the body responsible for delivering the government's sport objectives in schools. The school is involved in the 'National Schools Competition Framework' which promotes competitive sport in and between schools.

In addition, schools will often have their own logo, and also a motto or a vision statement. If a logo is a coat of arms and the motto in Latin, then either the school is one which has a long tradition, or it is trying to give that impression. A Latin motto might also imply an academic bias in the school. Some mottos can use language that is deliberately inclusive, and clearly is intended to emphasise that all achievement is celebrated, for example, 'We all succeed', while others might emphasise selection, 'What we do, we do better'. It is quite common for a school that is a specialist Language College to have a motto in a foreign language.

Exam Results

A school should include in their prospectus Key Stage test results, and the results of GCSE*, vocational qualifications, such as GNVQ* and 'A/S' and 'A' Levels*, if appropriate. These results will be for the most recent year, and there should be an analysis of relevant data for the last three or four years.

The most important information for a parent is what the exam results reveal about adding value; how much the school has done to help students to achieve their potential. However, most schools do not give their value added* information with their exam results, instead they usually focus on raw percentages, so it is often a question of reading between the lines to judge a school's success.

It is important to check the match between the quality of the brochure and the quality of the results. For example, a brochure might be glossy and impressive, but the results disappointing. In this instance, the quality of the brochure will have no effect on your child's experience at the school, but the quality of the results will.

Normally schools include national averages with which to compare their own achievements. If a school scores higher than the national averages, then that is clearly encouraging. However, this is not the end of the story. One of the most important considerations is that there is year on year improvement. If a school has results that are consistently higher than the national average, but there is no year on year improvement, then there may be some issues for you to explore.

By contrast, if a school is moving closer and closer to the national average year on year, or increasing their improvement upon it, then these are good signs. If schools do not include comparative data then the quality of their own examination analysis is questionable.

Key Stage 4 Examinations – GCSEs/GNVQS/BTECS

The table for the most recent GCSE results will usually have all the subjects down the left hand side, the grades along the top, the numbers of students who achieved each grade, and the total number of students who were entered for each subject down the far right column. Along the bottom column will be the total number of students who achieved each grade across all subject areas.

If you receive the prospectus in the Autumn term, GCSE grades for the most recent cohort are often indicated to be provisional because the school might be challenging some of the results or awaiting definitive DfES figures.

The comparative data will include information such as the percentage of students who achieved five or more A*–C grades, the number of students who achieved five or more A*–G grades, the number of students who achieved at least one GCSE and similar combinations. The comparative information can also be found in national Achievement and Assessment Tables*.

At Key Stage 4, it is compulsory for all students to study English, Maths and Science, Information Technology, Religious Education, Citizenship and Physical Education. However, not all schools will enter students for exams in all these areas. Most schools will enter all of their students for English, English Literature, Maths and Science GCSEs. Some schools will enter their students for half award GCSEs, for example, in Religious Education, Citizenship, and Information Technology. Most schools will not enter all their students for Physical Education GCSE.

Students will either be entered for dual award Science GCSE, which counts for two GCSEs, Science GNVQ/BTEC or three individual Science GCSEs (Physics, Chemistry and Biology). In some schools, other subjects will be compulsory for the whole year group, for example, a foreign language. Some schools enter all their students for the same GNVQ/BTEC, most commonly in ICT.

Results in compulsory subjects may tell a different story to those in option subjects. For example, nearly all students will be entered for Maths GCSE, whether they are strong or struggle in this subject, and the results will reflect this. However, if students opt for a subject, it is usually because they have some aptitude or enthusiasm for it. Option cohorts are almost always smaller than compulsory cohorts, so it is more likely that results will be higher in option subjects.

Schools will usually include vocational results in the same table as their GCSE results. BTEC will imminently become the most common vocational qualification. Year 11 students will normally achieve two GCSE equivalent qualifications; the more successful equating to grades A*–C at GCSE, others being comparable to grades D–G. With all GCSE data, national averages should accompany school totals.

Always have a calculator with you when you are looking at the data in a prospectus.

Example of GCSE tables in School Prospectus

SUBJECT	*	A	B	C	Total	D	E	F	G	U	N/A	CAND
English Lang.	2	7	2	61	72	26	30	8	2			138
English Lit.	2	6	36	28	72	33	24	9	4			142
Media Studies	1	2	3	2	8	5	5	3			1	22
TOTAL	5	15	51	91	162	74	59	20	6	5	1	327
Maths			26	39	65	35	37	16	9	5		167
Science		6	12	74	92	54	72	52	14	4		288

	4	3	2	1	0	99	98
ACHIEVING AT LEAST 5 GRADE "G"	82	86	88	86	86	94	92
ACHIEVING 5 "A*" TO "C" GRADES	30	24	33	35	33	35	25
ACHIEVING AT LEAST 1 GRADE "C"	60	68	67	55	59	66	55
ACHIEVING AT LEAST 1 GRADE "G"	90	90	94	88	91	98	97

Causes for Concern in GCSE/ Key Stage 4 Data

- The data in the prospectus should be set out in a way that is accessible to a parent audience. If it is not even clear that the table is about GCSE results; if there are abbreviations that are impossible to understand; if there are numbers and percentages that have no context; then this is *a cause for concern*. The school should be making an effort to communicate effectively with its audience through its use of data. If it cannot make its data parent friendly, it is highly likely that in classrooms, it does not make its data student friendly either.

- Most schools offer English Language, English Literature, Maths and Science as core GCSEs, which means all students take these subjects. Schools which do not offer English *and* English Literature, or offer a subject instead of English Literature for example, Media Studies, are reducing their students' entitlement. Subjects should not be taught instead of English and English Literature, but as well as.

- Across all the subjects, if there are more children who get 'D's than 'C's, then this suggests that the school could be failing students. Schools should be targeting students who are on the 'C/D' borderline and moving their grades up. One of the hardest things for a school to achieve, but one of the strongest signs of its success is to move students from 'D' to 'C'.

- Across all the subjects, if there are few students who achieve grades A* or A then this shows that the school does not serve its gifted and talented community well. It does not matter who the student cohort are, there will always be young people who are capable of 'A' grades.

- If the percentage of students (note – not the number) in the 'A*–C' columns in option subjects, for example, History or Geography is generally the same as, or lower than the core subjects (English, Maths and Science) this is not a good sign.

- If there is a subject area that has the majority of students on a 'D' grade or lower, then this subject could be *a cause for concern*. Most schools, no matter how good they are, will usually have one subject area where things may have gone wrong. Or, they have a subject area which attracts a disproportionate number of lower ability students. However, schools should not have more than two subject areas where most students achieve a 'D' or lower. If your child's favourite subject is an area where students are potentially underachieving in this way, then you will need to investigate the reasons why before you choose the school.

- In the comparative statistics showing the percentage of students achieving at least five or more 'A*–C' grades each year, there should not be a decrease over time. A downward trend suggests a school on a decline. Where there is no discernible trend either upwards or downwards, then this is *a cause for concern*, because it suggests that there is no effective strategy for improvement in place.

- If the percentage of students achieving least

one 'A*–G' grade each year, is not in the high 90s, then the school is not supporting its lowest ability students well enough. It might be concentrating on another group of students at the expense of those with lower academic ability.

- If the percentage of five or more 'A*–C' grades is going up, but the percentage of students achieving five or more 'A*–G' grades is going down, then the school may be focusing on higher ability students at the expense of those with lower ability.
- Some schools might not include a subject breakdown at GCSE level. This is not necessarily a cause for concern, but you should request this information before considering the school seriously.

Good Signs in GCSE/ Key Stage 4 Data

- It is a good sign if schools include a written explanation of their results. Paragraphs that explain particular achievements in different subject areas and individual achievements of students reveal a school that is serious about making their data comprehensible to parents.
- If you look down the grade columns 'C' and 'D' and the numbers are for the most part greater in 'C' than they are in 'D', then it is likely that the school is good at helping students reach their potential. This pattern suggests the school has a high success rate at converting students who could be 'D' graders into 'C' graders.
- If, in the majority of subject areas, more

students get 'B's and 'C's than any other grade, then this shows that the school is probably very good at adding value and getting the most out of their students. It also means that the school does not just concentrate on getting 'C' grades to do well in the Achievement and Assessment Tables, but pushes students beyond the 'C' boundary and further upwards

- There should be consistency across the option subjects and consistency across the core. So the percentages (note – not the number) of students at each grade should be broadly similar across core subjects and roughly the same across option subjects. This shows that there are consistent whole school systems contributing to school improvement, and progress is not just happening in isolated pockets.

- A spread of students across the 'A*–E' grade columns, without a bulge at 'D' or 'E', suggests that the school does its best for students of all abilities.

- There should be A*s and As in all subject areas. This indicates that the school is appropriately challenging its gifted and talented students.

- In the comparative statistics showing the percentage of students achieving five or more 'A*–C' grades each year, there should be an upward trend over time. Do not worry if the pattern is not totally consistent. A reduction of a few percentage points one year is not a cause for concern, but the trend should be upwards. This shows that it is an improving school.

- In the statistics showing the percentage of students achieving at least one 'A*–G' grade each year, the percentage should be in the high 90s year on year.

GCSE/Key Stage 4 Data in Grammar Schools.

- There should not be subject areas that have their highest number of students attaining a 'D' grade.
- In the majority of subject areas, the biggest number of students should be attaining a 'B' grade.
- There should be a large minority of students who achieve 'A*'s and 'A's in all subject areas, because gifted and talented students are a large proportion of the student cohort.

'AS/A' Level/Key Stage 5 Data

Usually, 'A' Level results are not parents' top priority, when they are thinking about which secondary school to choose. However, results in the 6th form can give you some guide to the school overall.

- It is *a cause for concern* if the school uses statistics that are not comprehensible. For example, they might include the average point score* without explaining what this tells the parent. This shows no attempt on the part of the school to give parents a clear picture of what is happening.

- A year on year improvement in results is a good sign.
- Results that show, in the majority of subjects, that most students get below a 'C' grade at 'A' Level are *a cause for concern*. This suggests that the school has a 6th form that is not actually for the benefit of the students, and/or that the students are underachieving, and might do better elsewhere.
- If the majority of subjects have a bulk of students attaining 'C' grades or above at 'A' Level, then this suggests a healthy 6th form.

AS/'A' Level/Key Stage 5 Data in Grammar Schools

- There should be very few 'E's and 'U's in any subject area. If these grades occur, students could be being encouraged to do the wrong 'A' Levels or 'A' Level teaching in some subject areas may be weak.
- A substantial minority of 'A' grades in all subject areas indicates good teaching and appropriate challenge

Key Stage 3 Data

There are national SATs tests at Key Stage 3 for English, Maths and Science. There will be two sets of results published by the school, one for teacher assessments and one for the tests themselves. Teacher assessments are the levels the teacher gives to students for the work they have done in class. The test result refers to the levels the students achieve in national externally marked tests.

Example of Key Stage 3 SATs table in School Prospectus

KS3		N	2	3	4	5	6	7	8	5+
English %	Teacher Assess.		14	29	31	24	1			56
	Test	1	3	10	14	45	18	3		66
	National	1	3	9	16	34	24	10		66
Maths %	Teacher Assess.			1	15	22	34	11		68
	Test	5	5	8	15	16	30	19	1	66
	National	1	2	5	16	26	22	19	5	73
Science %	Teacher Assess		4	13	40	20	17	1		39
	Test	6	4	6	24	28	29	3		60
	National	1	2	6	18	29	28	11		68

- Key Stage 3 SATs, are levelled from 2 to 8, while 'N' is awarded to students who failed to attain a level 2. At Key Stage 3, the nationally expected result for a child of 14 is level 5. Schools should include national average comparisons in their data.
- Schools are required to give their students a level at Key Stage 3 for all subject areas, although English, Maths and Science are the only subjects externally examined. Most schools will ensure that their levels in non-core subject areas are similar to the national averages, so these levels provide a parent with little new information.
- In English, Maths and Science, the number of students at each level for the teacher assessment should be broadly similar to the numbers for the test. If there is a significant gap between the test result and the teacher assessment in

each core subject, this suggests that the teachers do not have accurate assessment skills, which is not good news for your child.

- The percentage of students achieving level 5 or above should be broadly the same in English, Maths and Science. If it is not, this indicates that there could be a weak core subject area. It also suggests that whole school systems for ensuring improvement are not strong, and too much is left to the individual subject areas.

- In the tests, the majority of pupils should achieve a level 5 or above. This normally suggests that the school is adding appropriate value.

- In all schools, at Key Stage 3 there should be a smattering of level 7s and 8s in the three core subject areas. If this is not the case, then the school is failing its gifted and talented students.

Key Stage 3 Data – Grammar schools

- The number of students attaining level 4 in the three subject areas should be negligible.
- The number of students attaining a level 6 should be more than those achieving a level 5.
- There should be a large minority of students who achieve levels 7 and 8.
- There should be no weak subject – English, Maths and Science should be achieving at approximately the same levels.

Case Study

A friend of mine brought me the prospectus of a school that she was considering for her daughter. The appearance of the publication was impressive. It was printed on high quality paper, and had plenty of photographs. My friend's daughter is mixed race, and my friend was anxious that she went to a school which celebrated multi-culturalism. We were heartened by the choice of photographs, revealing a diverse school community, engaged in a variety of activities, academic, vocational and extra-curricular.

We appreciated the Head teacher's address. It was friendly and mentioned how much the school celebrated and valued the diverse needs of its student cohort. My friend was anxious that the school was 'strict' so was pleased to see how the enforcement of uniform rules was mentioned, along with a clear behaviour code, and high expectations of politeness.

As her daughter is musical, my friend was encouraged to find that the school was an Arts and Media College, and was impressed by the regular school productions staged. We both felt it was a promising touch that the prospectus included a glowing review from the local paper of the latest production, 'The Little Shop of Horrors'.

However, the enclosed data told a potentially different story to the one narrated in the text of the prospectus. In the results from the current year, there were no 'A*' or 'A' grades in Art, Music or Drama, which suggested that the gifted and talented in these areas were being short changed, even though the school was an Arts and Media College. It was also a cause for concern that over half of the cohort for GNVQ Performing Arts did not pass.

In Science the number of students at grade 'D' was twice as many as at 'C', which suggested that this subject was not good at moving students up from the 'C/D' borderline, and did not add enough value, particularly because this pattern was not reflected in English and Maths. My friend and I were concerned about sending her daughter to a school where the child apparently did not have an equal chance of reaching her potential in all three core subjects.

It was also noticeable that compared to the Arts subjects, the Humanities appeared to do much better. For example, in History, a quarter of all students achieved 'A' grades. This again suggested that the school's Arts and Media specialist status was misleading.

To sum up:
A prospectus must seem consistent, and have a clear sense of audience. It should be easy to access for parents. Be impressed but do not be seduced by high finish; the school itself must match up to the image. The exam data included can give you a picture of the school, if you look for particular patterns and trends.

Easy Guide

Prospectus – Exam Results

The school prospectus is the subject of the previous section. Most prospectuses contain a table of exam results. Here is a sample table broken down into sections with explanations of all the highlighted areas.

SUBJECT	*	A	B	C	Total	D	E	F	G	U	N/A	CAND
English Lang.	2	7	2	61	72	26	30	8	2			138
English Lit.	2	6	36	28	72	33	24	9	4			142
Media Studies	1	2	3	2	8	5	5	3			1	22
TOTAL	5	15	51	91	162	74	59	20	6	5	1	327
Maths			26	39	65	35	37	16	9	5		167
Science		6	12	74	92	54	72	52	14	4		288

Good Signs

In core subjects – higher number of students at 'C' than 'D', which is an indication that the school adds value and moves students up from the 'C/D' border-line.

Causes for Concern

Core subjects should have similar attainment levels. Here the totals are for Science 144 (½ of 288), 138 for English and 167 for Maths. In English and Science it may be the case that lower ability students are not doing well enough to be entered for the exam.

In Maths no A* or A grades – gifted and talented students are underachieving.

SUBJECT	*	A	B	C	Total	D	E	F	G	U	N/A	CAND
Geography			1	2	3	2	7	12	13	9		46
History	3	4	8	9	24	15	9	9	6	1		64
TOTAL	3	4	9	11	27	17	16	21	19	10		110

Causes for Concern

In Geography numbers increase as the grades go down – it may be that this subject is being badly taught and the students underachieve or it is a sink subject where students are placed who cannot achieve anywhere else.

In History there is a higher number of students at 'D' than at 'C' grade – it may be that staff do not have the subject knowledge and motivational skills to maximise 'C' grades.

SUBJECT	*	A	B	C	Total	D	E	F	G	U	N/A	CAND
Child Dev.	1	1	1	7	10	5	2	3	1			21
Food					3	2	3	2	3			13
Design & Tech.	1	8	11	35	55	33	27	16	11	6	2	150
Manufacturing				2	2	10		8				20
TOTAL	2	9	12	44	70	50	32	29	15	6	2	204

Causes for Concern

In Food the statistics do not make sense, there are no A*–Cs to give a total of 3.

The total of 70 does not add up.

SUBJECT	*	A	B	C	Total	D	E	F	G	U	N/A	CAND
Information Technology		6	53	151	210	17	19	9	1	27	6	289
Business Studies				2	2	4	6	4	2	6		24
TOTAL		6	53	153	212	21	25	13	3	33	6	313

Good Signs

Students do well in IT – significantly higher numbers of 'C's than 'D's.

Cause for Concern

Business Studies is seriously underperforming.

BEST INDIVIDUAL PERFORMANCE									
GIRLS					BOYS				
	*	A	B	C		*	A	B	C
EM	4	5	1.5		MB		3	2	6
ES	2	4	4	2.5	RW		2	2	7
CD	2	4	5		JT	1	1	4	3
MW	2	3	4	2	DU		2	1	8

Causes for Concern

Abbreviations without explanations.

Gifted and talented boys are not being stretched.

	4	3	2	1	0	99	98
ACHIEVING AT LEAST 5 GRADE "G"	82	86	88	86	86	94	92
ACHIEVING 5 "A*" TO "C" GRADES	30	24	33	35	33	35	25
ACHIEVING AT LEAST 1 GRADE "C"	60	68	67	55	59	66	55
ACHIEVING AT LEAST 1 GRADE "G"	90	90	94	88	91	98	97
ACHIEVING GRADE "A*" TO "C"	46	42	47	41	39	39	31

Causes for Concern

No explanation that the figures are percentages.

No explanation that the columns 4–98 represent years.

Over a five year period, the percentage of 'at least 5 grade 'G'' students and 'at least 1 grade 'G'' students is declining. This suggests that lower ability students are being let down.

Evaluation of Sample School

This would probably not be your first choice of school because:

- The school has not presented the data in a way that is intelligible to parents, with omissions of basic explanations.
- There are data inaccuracies, demonstrating a lack of attention to detail.
- There are clear indications to suggest the school is not adding value.

- Lower and higher ability students appear to be underachieving.
- Although the overall trend of students achieving five or more A*–C grades is one of some improvement, the improvement is slight and inconsistent.

The School Profile

The School Profile* replaces the governors' Annual Report. It is a new requirement for schools. The government's purpose in introducing the profile is to give parents useful and accessible information regarding the school's strengths and areas for improvement.

All schools must have completed their profile for 2004/5 by August 2006, and the 2005/6 profile by autumn 2006. Schools will then be required to update their profile annually.

The Head teacher is given a series of section headings for which he has a word limit. The headings are:

- What have been our successes this year?
- What are we trying to improve?
- How have our results changed over time?
- How are we making sure that every child gets teaching to meet their individual needs?
- How do we make sure our pupils are healthy, safe and well-supported?
- What activities are available to pupils?
- What have pupils told us about the school, and what have we done as a result?
- How do we make sure all pupils attend their lessons and behave well?
- What do our pupils do after year 11?
- What have we done in response to Ofsted*?
- How are we working with parents and the community?

The other sections are completed by the DfES*.

These are:

- How do our absence rates compare to other schools?
- How much progress do pupils make between 11 and 16?
- How well do our pupils achieve in year 11?
- How well do our pupils achieve at age 14?

• The profile can be accessed by anyone, through the parent centre website at www.schoolprofile.parentscentre.gov.uk.
• Although it replaces the governors' Annual Report, this will commonly be a document authored by the Head teacher.
• Both the School Profile and the prospectus are used by the Head teacher to promote the school. However, the profile does force the school to focus on areas for improvement and responses to Ofsted reports, and so it cannot be seen as solely a promotional vehicle.
• A lot of the information required in the profile is duplicated elsewhere in the prospectus, the Achievement and Assessment Tables* and the Ofsted report. However, the profile has the advantage of summarizing key information in the section 'How much progress do pupils make between 11 and 16?' The profile is much briefer than an Ofsted report and published more regularly.

Areas of the profile that are the most useful:

- What have been our successes this year?

Every school will represent their results in a positive light whatever the actual achievement. More revealing is what other areas the Head teacher chooses to focus on as this will tell you what the school priorities are.

– What are we trying to improve?

Every school should be looking to improve student performance, no matter how good their results are. You are looking for a degree of honesty here, an acknowledgement that improvement is needed. It is *a cause for concern* if the school blames other agencies for improvement issues, such as the LEA*.

– How much progress do pupils make between 11 and 16?

The progress measure is value added* so this diagram is useful. The category 'broadly average' is a large one, so it would be *a cause for concern* if the school came into any category lower than this. If the school is 'above average' or higher then this is a very good sign.

In the commentary by the side of the diagram, a score of 1000 or over means that the school is in the top half of the 'broadly average' category, and has added value during the last year.

– How are we working with parents and the community?

Parents' evenings, governor representation, academic review days*, reports, contact with Heads of

Year* are amongst the processes you would expect to find here. It is a good sign if a PTA* is mentioned, likewise parent surveys. Vague statements such as 'we work with the community in a number of different ways' without examples give no insight. Details on local projects and working links demonstrate that the school has a genuine community role.

– What activities are available to pupils?

There should be substantial content here. Look for activities that are clearly run on a regular basis, and are not one offs.

– What have pupils told us about the school, and what have we done as a result?

If there is a school council it should be mentioned here, and if specific examples of its impact are mentioned, then this is a good sign. Further examples of pupil consultation with reference to specific findings and resulting actions shows the school takes its student voice seriously.

– How do our absence rates compare with other schools?

This information can also be found in the Assessment and Assessment Tables and sometimes in the prospectus. If the table shows that the school's rates are higher than the local authority's and the national rates, year on year, then this is *a cause for concern*. Increasing absence rates year on year would suggest a school in decline. Look for a year on year reduction, or at least maintenance, of a similar rate.

– What have we done in response to Ofsted?

This section is only of interest if it includes specific areas identified by Ofsted and detailed responses.

To sum up:
School Profiles are in their early stages, and it is difficult as yet to assess what their usefulness will be. However, they do summarise data found in other lengthier sources of information and should give an insight into schools' evaluations of their own effectiveness.

Further Information
Achievement and Assessment Tables
Give you more detailed information on a school's exam results.
Ofsted Reports
Give you more detail and comment upon: meeting a child's individual needs, pupil well-being, extra-curricular activities and community links, behaviour and achievement from an impartial, external viewpoint.
Open Evening
Make sure the profile matches up with the reality.
School Prospectus
At present contains much of the information that is likely to be in the profile, for example, a detailed breakdown of exam results, attendance percentages, and an analysis of student destinations post 16.

Chapter 3 – The Detail

'The School'

Buildings and Environment

School buildings often look surprisingly shabby, and successful schools do not always have the most up to date buildings. A school that looks state of the art will not necessary mean it offers the best deal for your child.

- Good schools will make the most of their environment, and will exploit all opportunities to present good display to support learning. Rooms will appear organised and stimulating.
- Schools which have clearly thought about how environment stimulates learning are worth giving consideration to. It should be evident that the school's creative departments, for example, Art and Technology, have been involved in developing an inspiring environment throughout the building.
- Decoration decisions should take into consideration the promotion and celebration of learning, and not just the caretaker's favourite

colour. Decoration should clearly be a curriculum issue for a school. For example, a Maths corridor whose decoration celebrates numbers or a French corridor that alludes to languages is not hard to achieve.

- Graffiti will occur in all schools. However, it is a good sign if schools have a zero tolerance attitude. Most schools will have a real purge on graffiti for open evening, but what you need to find out is what the situation is like day to day. If graffiti is constantly cleaned off, then students will soon stop doing it, and learn to take pride in their environment.

- A set of buildings which give students a sense of ownership is more likely to lead to a happy school. There should be displays which instil a feeling of community, for example, artwork which portrays the students themselves, or is created by students collaboratively. It is worth finding out whether students have been involved in decisions about the school environment.

- You should look out for spaces which show that the institution respects and values its students. The eating area, for example, should be well maintained and student friendly. There should be pleasant places for the students to sit and congregate outside. There may be a garden cultivated by the students themselves.

- A school should be welcoming to visitors with a reception area that is accommodating to all its client groups, and that has had some time and money invested in it.

- The office staff should be professional and

friendly. The office is a good indication of the ethos of the whole school.

- It is always a nice touch if students are used as monitors to welcome visitors and run errands.
- It is a good idea to find out whether students are allowed in the building at break and lunchtimes and if not, why not. It is *a cause for concern* if they are not trusted in the building.
- The right school for your child should be recently decorated. It does not cost much to keep an interior freshly decorated, and it shows that the school is valued by those who work in it.
- All secondary schools are involved in the government programme Building Schools for the Future, BSF*. The aim is to rebuild or renew every secondary school in England over the next 10-15 years. A small number of schools have gone through the process, most are waiting for their turn.
- It is important to find out where the school you are considering stands with regard to building work. The positive effects of building work can be long term. Whilst the building is taking place, there are often discipline and behaviour issues, because there are suddenly lots of tempting, dangerous places that are no go areas for the students. Usually, if students are put up in temporary accommodation for any length of time, behaviour management and quality of learning issues can develop. Learning can suffer if pupils are temporarily re-housed in unfamiliar rooms. If your school of choice has a building programme planned, you need to be confident that it will be managed in

the students' best interests.
- New builds are usually very popular with parents. However, it is important to remember that buildings do not in themselves make good schools.

Further Information
Informal Visit
Pop into the school on a pretext, ask for the prospectus, or ask when their open day is, even if you know already. It is important that you feel you are treated respectfully and professionally.
Visit
Make sure you see the school in the daylight. This is another good reason to go on a tour during the day. Often, on open evenings, you get no real sense of the school's outdoor space because it is dark outside.

Case Study
In B School, the Head teacher had just taken over a building whose interior décor was dilapidated. The school had been without a permanent Head for a year and a half and was in serious weaknesses*. Graffiti was common and was not cleaned off regularly. The school had not been freshly painted for a long time, and most rooms, even when there was good display, had a scruffy feel to them. The buildings were only about 30 years old so it was not their age that had let the place down.

One of the first things the Head teacher did was to take better care of the environment, to show students that where they worked was an important place to be, and was valued highly. He gave an Art teacher the responsibility to enter the school for any competition that would result in some sort of make over. He took five of the most difficult students in one year group and worked with them to design the decoration for the dining hall. In the end the students were working voluntarily out of school hours to repaint it, when previously it was difficult to keep them in school for a whole lesson at once. The Head teacher overhauled the reception with new carpet and used different students each day as receptionists to welcome visitors. They very rarely abused their position. He gave the Librarian £100 to make over a patch of grass outside the library back door. She soon had a set of library helpers who created a student garden.

Within six weeks, graffiti was dramatically reduced, behaviour around the school was much improved, the dining hall was more peaceful, and a greater number of students used the library.

To sum up:
The right school for your child might not be the school with the most impressive site. It is how it adapts its environment for learning that counts.

Facilities and Resources

There are standard resources that all schools should have. For example, all secondary schools should have established the ratio of one computer for every five students by August 2004. However, some schools will have more extensive resources than others because of additional sources of income, for example, specialist* status or Excellence in Cities* funding. Resources can certainly impact upon a school's achievements but do not in themselves guarantee success. The key for parents is to judge how well schools make use of their resources.

- Specialist* schools receive an extra sum per pupil annually over five years and a one off capital grant of £150,000 to dedicate to their specialist area.
- If schools have an active PTA*, they often have extra resources acquired through its fund-raising.
- Some schools will share facilities with partners, such as leisure centres. Others can use off site facilities like local swimming pools.
- Sometimes a child will want to go to a school because of what the resources look like. For example, boys are often wooed by schools which are attached to leisure centres, because they have extensive sports' facilities. However, the sports' facilities might not have much impact on the success of the school as a whole, or even, for that matter, the success of the PE department. It is often facilities which provoke most argument between parents and their children over which school is the best to choose.
- Location impacts upon resources. Inner city schools often suffer from a lack of outside space, with a consequent impact upon the taught curriculum and after school activities like sports clubs. Schools in less urban areas may have more land and be able to offer a wider

variety of after school sports activities on site.

- If basic resources are missing, like new books in the library, or CD players in the Languages Department then this is *a cause for concern*. Such deficiencies may indicate that the school has serious financial management issues and, if this were the case, it would not be the right place for your child.

- If your child has a particular interest in a subject which relies on extensive resourcing, then it is important to take this into consideration. For example, if your child loves Photography, it would be ideal if the school had a dark room and a Photography club. Similarly, if their specialism is Music, look out for a well equipped music suite. A specialist school whose specialism matches your child's interests could be a school to consider seriously, because their resources in that particular area should be extensive.

Further Information
Open Evening/Visit
Make sure you view resources, particularly in subjects your child has a special interest in. Remember, there may be some additional facilities that the school has access to that are not on site.

To sum up:
The school of your choice needs satisfactory resources. However, it is essential to ensure that the learning environment is inspiring, resources don't guarantee results.

School Library

A good school library can facilitate effective learning.

- A school librarian who is enthusiastic and interacts with students can have a significant effect on the quality of their learning.
- The more a child reads and enjoys reading, the easier they will find all studying, because their literacy skills are likely to be good. A good library should have lots of programmes and schemes on offer to entice students to read.
- A good librarian will know what books will encourage students into the library, and promote these in the school.
- A school that is right for your child will have a library which is an attractive place to be. Displays will be stimulating and up to date.
- Students often underachieve because they do not have a good learning space at home. A school library should be a place where children can learn effectively including before and after lessons.
- A good library should be up to date with appropriate technologies and media, for example, computers, scanners and printers. These should be well maintained.
- The best test of a school library is if it is well used for the right purpose. It is *a cause for concern* if it looks good, but no student goes into it. It is no good if the librarian is allergic to children. It is *a cause for concern* if students only visit the library when it is raining at break times.

- A good library hooks up with the taught curriculum. Lessons will be taught there, books that subjects need will be available, staff will be regular users.
- A school that is right for your child should run a programme in their first year to show students how to use the library.
- A good library will be a sanctuary for students who want to work and explore learning. It will be a place where students feel safe and welcome.

Further Information
Open Evening/Visit
Visit the library and speak to the librarian. Ask her how well used the library is. Ask her what schemes she runs to encourage students to use the library. Ask her how many lessons actually take place in the library, and what subjects are taught there. It is *a cause for concern* if any of the computers have a 'Not In Use' sign.

During your visit ask the student showing you round about the library. Do they ever use it? Do they like it? What do they use it for? Make sure you go and see the library, see if students in there are working, or are they just sitting around and chatting.

Case Study
In P School there was a modern, well funded library. Displays were always kept up to date, new books were ordered regularly, the library environment was maintained immaculately. However, the librarian was scared of children. He refused to go

into any classes to present books, even with the class teacher present. He refused to run any pupil activities himself. He would not have a scheme of student librarians. He would not speak in assemblies, and was not confident to chase students up if they failed to return their books.

Therefore, the library was immaculate because it was never used. Students had no relationship with the librarian, so were not connected to the library. The only time the library was used was during wet breaks, when a member of the senior staff had to go and turn disruptive students out, because the librarian could not deal with them.

In P School, had the library been removed completely, I am convinced there would have been no lowering of attainment among students, and very few people would have noticed any difference, apart from the librarian.

To sum up:
A good library can be a real asset to a school. However, to have any effect on your child's education, it must be well and appropriately used by students.

School Meals

At the time of writing, there has been much recent media debate about the quality of food students receive at school. It is true that a school's catering arrangements can influence the behaviour of students and their achievement in lessons. It is something you will want to take into consideration when choosing the right school for your child.

- In secondary schools, the canteen can either be run by the LEA* catering service, a private contractor, or by the school itself.
- There have undoubtedly been issues with some private catering firms, which have allegedly put profit before quality when catering for children.
- However, some arrangements between schools and private caterers have been tremendously successful, often because the caterer has had the funding to promote the food so that students stay in school to eat it.
- The right school for your child will have made connections between the performance of their students and the food that they eat. For example, some schools ensure that there are no drinks on sale in their canteen with additives which could induce hyper-activity in young people.
- Some schools, particularly those which manage catering themselves, have established healthy eating practices.
- The success of a school's food provision depends in part on the quality and size of their site. If they have a spacious site, then they can afford to keep all students on the premises at lunchtimes, and therefore have greater control over what children eat. If they have a small site, then they may have to allow students off site at lunchtimes. In this case, schools have little control over what students eat, as children will always prefer the local burger bar to anything, whatever its quality, that is provided in the school canteen.

- A school's lunchtime is often when the atmosphere appears most unstable. This is because students can be difficult to supervise during a long lunch interval and, apart from a few senior staff, supervision is usually carried out by midday assistants* who do not have the authority and the training of teachers.
- If a school has an adequately sized dining room, it is likely that their eating arrangements will be more civilised.
- If a school has made the eating area appealing, and somewhere where students can relax, then it is likely that eating arrangements will be more civilised.
- If a school is accredited as a Healthy School* this shows they are taking healthy eating seriously.
- A school that is serious about improving its catering will involve parents and students in their decision making.
- Some schools have contracts with companies to provide vending machines on site. Often what is provided by these machines is not what parents would consider healthy food.
- A canteen that is trying hard to attract students will have a range of choices, snacks at break times, hot and cold meal options, sandwiches and full meals.
- All schools should have a Food Technology* Department. The right school for your child will have links between this department and school catering to ensure that what students learn about food in lessons informs what food is provided for them at meal times.

- The take up rate for meals is a good indication of how hard a school is trying to cater appropriately for students. If most students eat out of school, or bring a packed lunch, then these are not good signs. It is a very good sign if staff eat in the canteen, because they are usually more interested in healthy food than the students and usually have more opportunities than the students to eat elsewhere.

  Also, if staff not only get their food from the canteen but eat there as well, rather than taking their food to the staff room, then the canteen atmosphere will normally be more inclusive and relaxed.

- The government provides free school meals* to students whose parents access benefits. The percentage of students eligible for free school meals is often used as a gauge to assess the level of deprivation amongst a school's cohort.

- Some schools have imaginative eating arrangements to facilitate a more pleasant lunchtime for students. For example, it is a common practice to split lunchtimes so that older students eat at a different time to younger students.

Further Information
Ofsted
The section 'Personal Development and Well-being' usually contains a comment on healthy eating.
Open Evening
Ask how many students have school dinners. Find out whether students are allowed out of school at lunchtime, and if they are, where do they usually eat.

Visit the Food Technology department; ask what connections they have with school catering.

Ask how many students the canteen holds at one time, and what system the school uses to get all the students through the canteen at lunchtime.

Ask how parents and students are involved in decisions about catering arrangements.

Prospectus

The prospectus should indicate whether the school has Healthy School status. Some schools' literature will contain an example of a day's menu.

School Profile

In the section 'What have been our successes this year?' or 'How do we make sure our pupils are healthy…' some Head teachers might comment on healthy eating initiatives.

Visit

Make sure you see the canteen. It should be designed in a way that is appealing to students. If possible, visit at lunchtime. This will give you a good insight into the atmosphere and attitude towards food. Is there material on display, for example, promoting healthy eating?

Ask the student showing you round what they think about school meals. Don't take their answer at face value. For example, they might love the food because it is always burgers and chips. Ask them what is actually on offer to students.

Ask them how many staff eat in the canteen.

To sum up:
Schools that take an interest in the food they serve to students are concerned about the 'whole' child, and this should influence your choice.

Uniform

There are a few non-uniform secondary schools but the vast majority have a uniform, certainly in Years 7–11.

- School uniform is a leveller. If everyone has to wear the same clothes, it reduces fashion competition. This makes many young people feel happier and more secure. However, within any uniform, there is always some peer pressure to conform to trends, such as brands of bag or coat.
- A uniform can reduce differences between students' economic backgrounds.
- It is a good sign if uniform rules are enforced. If a school adopts a uniform, but does not make their students wear it, this is *a cause for concern*. The institution is sending out the message to its students that rules can be flaunted. If students are allowed to rebel in small ways, for example, shirts hanging out, they may try to rebel in bigger ways as well.
- Uniform rules should be enforced by all staff, not just by some. Students should be expected to wear proper uniform throughout the school.
- It is a good sign if students wear their uniform with pride. This shows that the school pays attention to detail and that the children are proud of their uniform and their school. For example ties should be fastened.
- If a school adopts a uniform, it knows its students will be identified in the community. It is therefore doubly important that the school

enforces the uniform to maintain a good local reputation.

- There are of course different uniforms, which create varying messages. Schools that have blazers are often trying to establish or maintain a traditional, usually academic, ethos. Many successful schools have very well maintained uniforms but have abandoned ties, seeing them as untidy.

- Thoughtful uniform guidelines will take into consideration the religious and cultural mix of the school's intake. For example, if girls are allowed to wear skirt, trousers or shalwar kameez, then those students who wear the shalwar kameez do not stand out and feel fairly treated. However, if girls are only allowed to wear skirt or shalwar kameez, then faith differences, as identified by dress, become exacerbated.

- It can appear that some schools choose uniforms that are deliberately expensive, to influence the nature of their client group. For example, a school might demand apparently unnecessary duplication in their sports' kit, asking for a different piece of kit for each sport. Or, a school could demand different summer and winter uniforms.

- Some schools choose uniforms because they are distinctive, and although affordable, can only be brought from particular suppliers. This makes it easier to ensure that the uniform is adhered to.

- Some schools choose uniforms that are particularly accessible, for example a white polo shirt, so that they can guarantee all parents can easily find it.

- Some schools consult students when adopting or changing their uniform.
- Many schools facilitate the wearing of their uniform by selling clothing directly.
- Parents are often requested to sign up to the uniform policy. A good school should expect and receive support from its parents in enforcing the wearing of uniform.
- A few secondary schools do not have a uniform during Years 7–11. This suggests that the school has a libertarian approach to students' social development.

Further Information
Prospectus
Make sure you read the uniform policy carefully, understand and agree with it.
Informal Visit
Watch the students coming out of school at the end of the day – is the uniform code enforced? It does not matter if students are undoing their ties outside the gate, but it does matter if they are wearing uniform sloppily inside the grounds. If a significant number of students are out of uniform and nothing is done about it, then this is *a cause for concern*.
School Profile
In the section 'What have pupils told us about the school?' it might mention whether students have been consulted on uniform policy.

Case Study

A new Head teacher arrived at School L where achievement was being undermined by low level disruptive behaviour amongst a significant minority of students. There was a uniform code but it had been only loosely enforced by the previous Head. This had sent out the message to students that minor breaking of rules was acceptable and high expectations did not need to be met. The new Head teacher knew that to be successful, gain the respect of the students and challenge the school's tardy attitude he would have to address uniform straight away. Parents were all contacted and reminded about the uniform code. If the students did not possess the correct uniform, parents were given a short period of time to ensure that they did. The Head made sure that all items of the uniform except shoes were available at a discounted price at the office. Parents were told that after the allocated period of time had elapsed, students wearing incorrect uniform would be isolated. The Head teacher had complaints from parents, saying that this would jeopardise students' learning. He made it clear to parents that, in choosing the school, they had signed up to the uniform policy and therefore had to support it.

The Head held a series of assemblies explaining the new expectations to students. He explained how proud he was of them, so proud that he wanted them recognised on the streets because of their uniform. He made clear his expectations for students whenever and wherever they wore school uniform.

When it came to the week when full uniform was

to be enforced, only a tiny number of students were improperly dressed. Most students enjoyed their new smartness. Prizes were given to all tutor groups who came in perfect uniform for the whole week.

The senior team increased their lunchtime patrols outside school, so they could see how students were behaving in their uniform off site. They appeared in the most unexpected places and disruptive behaviour of any kind was rigorously followed up.

The Head teacher received far more letters from parents praising the enforcement of policy than condemning it. Local businesses contacted him about the improved behaviour of students. Students and staff knew that the new Head teacher meant business. The school was on the up.

To sum up:
Whatever the uniform code of the school, it is important that it is enforced; otherwise the institution sends a message out to its students that its rules can be undermined.

'The Classroom'

Assessment

The right school for your child must take its remit of raising achievement seriously. Therefore, all teachers must have a sound knowledge of how to assess what level or grade children are at, and possess the ability to help move students to a higher grade.

- In a school which is effective at raising achievement, all teachers will have a clear and up to date assessment record for every student they teach.
- Teachers should regularly share current performance and targets for improvement with every student.
- Teachers should regularly give students specific advice on the steps they must take to move up to the next grade.
- Teachers should write grades in exercise books when they mark, including guidance on what students must do to make progress.
- Schools should regularly share students' levels of achievement with their parents.
- Schools should assess students regularly, at least termly.
- Students should be well versed in what different levels of achievement mean. They should be able to explain levels of achievement in their own terms.
- Students should be able to explain to parents what they have to do to move on to the next

level or grade, and why they are not at that level or grade yet.

- Students should know what level of performance is expected for different age groups.
- No school, no matter how successful it is, will have practice which is equally good in all subject areas. However, ideally students should be aware of what levels they are at across the board, not just in, for example, the core subjects.

Further Information
Open Evening
Ask what kind of target setting the school does, and how it shares assessment information with students. Look out for assessment criteria appearing as part of classroom display. You should look to find this in every classroom.
Open Evening/Visit
Ask the student showing you round what level or grade they are working at in English, Maths and Science. Ask them what they need to do to reach the next level or grade. If the student cannot answer either of these questions, then this is *a cause for concern*.

Ask students what levels or grades they are working at in different subject areas. If there are one or two subject areas that they do not know, then this is not a particular worry. If they do not know what level they are working at for most of their subjects, then this is *a cause for concern*.
School Profile
Assessment might be mentioned under a variety of sections.

Case Study

A high ability student, Eve, joined School PH in Year 10. She was on course for grade Bs in English, but had the potential to achieve A*s. In English, her problem was not that she was lazy, or not bright enough. She had never achieved any higher than a B because she did not know what A* standard work looked like or how to achieve it. Her work so far had not been marked with appropriate targets on how to progress further. In her previous school, Eve just received ticks and 'excellents' on her work. In her new school's English lessons, she received clear and specific targets. Eve was given worksheets which explained what each grade meant and what she would have to do to achieve the next grade. She was given an assessment every month, which was graded with explanations as to why the work was at that grade, and what she had to do to move to a higher grade. Eve eventually achieved two A*s in her English GCSEs.

To sum up:

A good school will regularly tell your child where they are with their learning and give them clear and specific steps to improve.

Class Size

Smaller class sizes are often what parents pay for if they send their child to an independent* school. They are often quoted as one of the chief factors in raising attainment. Students can flourish in larger classes, if they are motivated and on task. However, it is undeniable that in smaller classes, students are likely to get more individual attention from the teacher and therefore more teacher input to their learning.

- The usual maximum secondary school class size is 30 students, nearer 20 in practical subjects like PE or Technology. It is *a cause for concern* if class sizes are commonly over 30. Some schools are able to staff lessons so that class sizes are smaller at Key Stage 4* in order to give students more individual support.
- Usually if a subject sets*, it will have larger classes for higher sets and smaller classes for lower sets. The rationale being that higher ability students do not need so much individual attention from teachers because they are more motivated and better at independent learning. This is something a parent should bear in mind if they have a child who is of high ability but is not a good independent learner or has a short attention span. In this situation, the child might not flourish in the set which is most appropriate to their academic ability because of the class size. Sometimes in a setting system, able students placed in lower sets, and who need more attention, flourish because of the smaller class sizes.
- At Key Stage 4, students select options. Often these classes are smaller than in the core subjects of English, Maths and Science.

Further Information
Open Evening
Ask about class sizes and how the needs of individual students are met within classes.

Ask about the class sizes different option subjects usually have, and how small does a group have to be before a school decides it is not viable to run that option. If the school sets or streams*, you need to find out how this affects class sizes.
Prospectus
The prospectus should tell you how big classes are in core and option subjects at Key Stages 3 and 4.
Visit
If the class sizes look small, make sure you ask why. You need to know if the reason for small size classes is truancy or other absences.

Case Study
Alicia came to School CH in Year 10 full of promise. Reports from her previous school and her SATs* results suggested that she would achieve five or more A*–C grades at Key Stage 4 without difficulty. However, she started going off the rails quickly, truanted, and her progress reduced dramatically. The only subject in which Alicia flourished was Spanish because there were only ten students in the class. Consequently, if she missed a lesson, it was easy for the teacher and her fellow pupils to fill her in on the missed work. Alicia was a very confident student, and in the group of ten had plenty of opportunity to practice her spoken Spanish, so she became fluent despite her frequent absences. Alicia achieved eight grade Ds in her GCSEs, apart from Spanish where she got an A grade. She got a job in

a travel agents, whose normal policy was to only take on students who had five or more A*–C grades, but because of her Spanish they made an exception for Alicia, so long as she retook her English and Maths GCSEs.

To sum up:
In state secondaries, there are important variations in class sizes between schools, which could impact upon the achievement of your child.

Curriculum

<u>Key Stage 3</u>

State schools follow the National Curriculum* at Key Stage 3 meaning their curriculum offer is fairly standard. However, there are some permitted variations which might influence your choice of school, taking into consideration your child's strengths and preferences.
The Key Stage 3 National Curriculum consists of:

English, Maths, Science, Design and Technology, Information and Communication Technology (ICT), History, Geography, Modern Foreign Languages (MFL), Art & Design, Music, PE, Citizenship, RE, Personal, Social and Health Education (PSHE).

- Most secondary schools offer Drama as a separate subject, but a minority incorporate it within English at Key Stage 3.
- Science is taught in various ways. At Key Stage

3 it is usually taught as integrated Science, but in more academic schools it can be split up into Biology, Chemistry and Physics. Technology is often broken down into different subjects, for example, Resistant Materials*, Food Technology* and Textiles*.

- The modern foreign language most schools offer in Year 7 is French. Sometimes, in Year 8 some students have the chance to take a second language, for example, Spanish.

- There is often a curriculum bias at Key Stage 3 in specialist* schools. For example a Language College might require all students to take two modern foreign languages.

- Some subjects are often taught through others. For example, you might find Photography within the Art curriculum.

- PSHE and Citizenship may not feature as separate subjects, but might be delivered through tutor time or assemblies.

- Like subjects are often grouped together. For example, Expressive and Performing Arts can include Art, Dance, Drama and Music. Humanities may include Geography, History, RE, Citizenship and PSHE.

- Sometimes subjects are offered on a termly carousel arrangement for example the combination of Art, Textiles and Graphics.

- Sometimes students study subjects in more depth, or even begin exam topics, in Year 9 to help them prepare for their Key Stage 4 courses.

- It is important to find out about grouping arrangements at Key Stage 3, whether subjects set, stream or teach in mixed ability groups.

- Remember to find out how students access any additional subjects offered in Years 8 or 9. For example, sometimes only students who are in the top set for French are offered a second modern foreign language.
- The variations that schools offer within the statutory requirements of the National Curriculum often depend on the expertise of the staff. For example an Art teacher's specialism might mean that a school can offer more Textiles or Photography.

Key Stage 4

English, Maths, Science, ICT, RE and PE are obligatory subjects in all schools at Key Stage 4. In most schools, however, they are not all examination subjects. English, Maths and Science certainly will be. However, individual schools will have differing arrangements for which of the other core subjects students are studied to examination level.

- Individual schools have a variety of additional compulsory subjects. For example, faith* schools normally have RE as a compulsory examination subject. A specialist Language College is likely to make at least one language compulsory
- If your child wishes to specialise in a subject at Key Stage 4* that is not part of the school's core offer, then it is important to find out whether this subject is regularly offered and if students are guaranteed a place on the course.
- Specialist schools are likely to have more Key

Stage 4 options in their specialist area than other schools which do not share their specialism.

- Often, because of staffing or curriculum changes, schools will have a popular option subject when your child arrives in Year 7 which may not exist by the time they reach Year 10.
- Most schools will not run an option subject if there is not enough take up from students.
- The range of vocational* options varies greatly from school to school. Some schools will offer two qualifications in one subject area, for example, both a GCSE and a BTEC* in Science. Sometimes, only high ability students can follow the GCSE in a subject area where there are two qualifications offered, and these same students cannot take the vocational option. Other schools leave the choice between vocational and academic courses up to the student and their parents.
- Some schools provide a skills based qualification, sometimes involving a college placement, at Key Stage 4 for students who might find it difficult to access the full examination curriculum.

Further Information
Open Evening
If your child is likely to be interested in a particular course at Key Stage 4 make sure the school will be running it when your child reaches Year 10. Find out what the eligibility is for each Key Stage 4 option. Find out what the school sees as a viable class size to run a Key Stage 4 option.

Prospectus

Check what the curriculum offer is for Key Stage 3. For example it might be that your child has been looking forward to taking Drama at secondary school but it is not offered as a separate subject until Year 9. Your child might be interested in the school because they offer Textiles, but they will only be able to access it one term per year.

Check what the Key Stage 3 grouping arrangements are and the selection criteria for any additional subjects on offer.

There will usually be a list of Key Stage 4 option subjects with their results. It is also worth finding out what the compulsory subjects are. You do not want your child saddled with a compulsory subject that you do not think is appropriate or useful.

School Publications

Ask for a copy of the option information for the current Year 9 group.

To sum up:

The Key Stage 3 curriculum might have variations that could motivate or discourage your child in their early years at school.

Key Stage 4 options influence further education and career choices. It is essential that you investigate them before deciding on your child's school.

Grouping Arrangements

Schools have differing arrangements for organising the way classes are taught. The most common arrangements are mixed ability*, setting*, a combination of the two, or streaming*.

Mixed ability is when students of varying abilities are taught in one class.

Setting is when students are grouped according to their ability by each individual subject.

Streaming is when students are put into the same ability group for all subjects.

There are ongoing ideological and practical debates about the benefits of each system. Studies can be found which 'prove' the benefits of all of them. At the time of writing, the present government is pro-setting and this is the arrangement used by most secondary schools. It is for parents to decide which system will be best for their child.

- A school which sets or streams could do so immediately in Year 7 using Key Stage 2* data from primary school, or after one term when it has carried out its own assessments. If this happens then parents must be confident that their child reached their potential in the Key Stage 2 SATs* examinations and that the secondary school has the results. If they under-achieved, a child could be labelled incorrectly at the start of their secondary school career, a position from which, academically, they might never recover.

- If a school sets or streams, it must have systems for a child to change their set or stream on the basis of ongoing performance. For example, a Maths department might have a test at the end of each half term to see if students are in the correct set. Parents need to be aware of what the arrangements for moving sets are. If a child is a late developer, and there are not mechanisms for them to change sets when they are ready, then the child could be trapped in groups which do not meet their needs.

- In setting systems, 'higher' groups usually have more students than 'lower' groups. Lower sets then can be better for students who have particular needs in a subject area, or flourish with greater teacher attention. Higher sets rely on students being well motivated learners who can learn independently in a large group. Parents must think carefully about how their child learns. For example, a child who is bright in Maths, but needs constant attention might not flourish in a setting environment.

- A streaming system is the most inflexible for children. If a child is wrongly placed in the middle stream and then moved to the upper stream, they will have to catch up in all subject areas. If a child is put in the wrong stream and not moved up, then all their subject areas will suffer. Parents must be confident that their child would be resilient in this system.

- If a school streams, it does not take into consideration the fact that a student might be very good at one subject and really struggle at another. Setting and mixed ability arrangements accommodate a greater variation of specialist ability in a child.

- Because of schools' ongoing pre-occupation with Achievement and Assessment Tables*, sometimes the best teachers teach the students who are most likely to get A*–C grades, and in a school that sets or streams, they are the students in the highest groups.

- In some schools lower sets can be 'sink' sets, where students with a range of issues, for example, behavioural concerns, learning difficulties, or problems with concentration levels, are placed so as not to impact on the progress of the majority.

- Students who are in the highest sets or streams are often motivated by being considered the 'top' students. Students in the lower sets or streams can be de-motivated by being in the 'bottom' sets, and sometimes do not improve because expectations of them are low.

- It is rare to find a school which teaches all subjects in a mixed ability environment. Often, in Year 7, the core* subjects are set and other subjects taught in mixed ability groups. Sometimes, Maths and Science are set and English is mixed ability. Usually there is less mixed ability teaching as the students move up the school and there is more focus on exams.

- Different children suit different grouping arrangements. For example, a bright boy who is a slow developer may be let down by setting. By the time his ideas mature, he will have been in lower sets for too long to make up the ground lost.

  A bright girl who is a fast developer and a hard worker will flourish in a setting system. She will be able to maintain her position in the top sets and be consistently challenged.

- Often, bright, well motivated and hardworking students benefit from setting. They are grouped with like minded children, and will flourish in the friendship groups formed by academic sets. In a setting arrangement, these students are likely to be free from taunts about their intelligence and work ethic.

- It is argued that mixed ability teaching can create a more inclusive classroom, where students of different abilities work together to the benefit of all. However, as a parent you would have to see this at first hand in the classroom to be convinced. In my experience, inclusion is an outcome of very good mixed ability teaching, not mediocre teaching. If your child works better in inclusive environments, that are potentially more nurturing and less competitive, then a mixed ability climate might be right for them.

- High ability students work well when they are encouraged to explain concepts to lower ability children. If your child enjoys working in this way, then you might want to consider mixed ability arrangements, as they are more likely to develop the students through having them 'teach' each other.

- Some schools use academic sets to determine option subject classes. For example, only students in top set for French may be allowed to choose two languages at Key Stage 4. Sometimes, students in top sets are precluded from taking option vocational subjects as the courses are deemed insufficiently academic.

If your child has a preference for a subject that is only taught from Year 10 onwards, it is important to find out what the arrangements for choosing that subject are. For example, it might be your child really wants to do Spanish, and a school you are considering only allows students in the top set for French to choose Spanish. If you feel it is unlikely that your child is going to make that top set position, then it might not be the right school for them.

Further Information
Open Evening
If the school does set, make sure it has clear systems for moving students up and down sets.
Open Evening/Visit
If the school sets, ask the students showing you round what sets they are in, how they feel about it and whether students ever move between sets.
Prospectus/Open Evening
Find out which subjects set, and which are taught in mixed ability classes. Find out if the school streams. Find out what data the school uses to determine what groups to put students in and when they establish these groups.

Case Study
In School TH students were set in Maths. Billy was a talented mathematician, but in his first year at secondary school, he did not reach his potential. He was lazy, and although he picked up concepts quickly, Billy could not be bothered to write things down and work methodically. Consequently, when students were put into sets after the first term, Billy found himself in set 3. At first he was motivated because he was easily top of the set, and could answer all of the questions faster than anybody else. However, after half a term, he lost his

enthusiasm because the pace of the class was too slow for him. The teacher gave Billy differentiated work to stretch him, but because he saw it as extra work, which the other students did not get, he never pushed himself. His attention span grew shorter, and he participated in more low level disruption.

By Year 10, Billy had matured, was able to apply himself and was no longer lazy. However, by this time, he had written Maths off because he was in the set 4, and rarely did any work. Billy decided to concentrate on his other subjects. When he had arrived at secondary school, he was predicted a B/C grade in Maths. In the end, he achieved an E.

To sum up:
Individual children are suited to different teaching arrangements, and this must be considered when choosing the right school for your child.

Homework

It is sometimes homework which really inspires a student's interest in a subject. The right school for your child will have effective homework systems.

- A good school will set homework which interests students, raises attainment and encourages independent learning. It will have systems to ensure that homework is completed.
- All good schools will have a homework policy. Ask to see it and find out if it represents reality.
- A successful school will make sure that home-

work is set in all subjects, and have high expectations for its completion.

- The right school for your child will make sure that homework is marked, valued, and used to raise attainment.

- If a school sets homework, it should have clear systems which come in to play when students do not complete the work set. For example, it might be school policy to set a detention every time homework is not completed.

- Homework may be set, but some students might not do it. If completing homework is not the rule, this may be *a cause for concern*. It suggests that the school does not have a strong work ethic.

- Homework should not be set for its own sake. It must be meaningful work, which should enhance learning in class.

- Homework must be possible for all to complete, otherwise it may be demoralising for students and exclude those without particular resources at home, for example, computers. Schools should have a clear system to support students if they do not understand the homework set or lack the resources to complete it.

- Homework should be differentiated according to ability.

- A supportive school will often have homework clubs to support students.

- Good schools will have a system to inform parents of homework set; through a journal*, through the school website or through the publication of homework schedules for parents.

- At the time of writing, a small number of

secondary schools are dispensing with home-work in its conventional form. This in itself is not necessarily a cause for concern, but a parent must investigate the reasons for this policy and be satisfied that traditional home-work is being compensated for in alternative ways.

Further Information
Open Evening
Choose a Head of Department* and ask about their homework policy. Ask to see some completed homework in their display of students' work.
Prospectus
Many prospectuses contain the school's homework policy. This is a good sign, but you must ensure at first hand that the policy is enacted.
School Publications
Phone the school and ask if they send out informa-tion to parents about homework. Ask if you can be sent the information they have distributed to parents during the last term. Ask if you can be sent a homework timetable for Year 7 students. This will show you whether the school has an overview of the homework being set. See if homework is kept up to date on the website.
Visit
Ask the student showing you round about home-work, how much they get and what happens to them if they don't complete it. Ask the student if they get much homework they do not understand. Ask them what they do if they do not understand it.

To sum up:
A good homework system helps your child to learn independently, and should be clearly and consistently applied.

'The People'

Diversity and Multi-culturalism

It is a common perception that the more ethnic minorities and home languages there are amongst a school's student population, the more demands will be placed on teachers, and the less individual help all students will receive. I have also heard English speaking parents claim, that in a school with lots of children who have English as a second language, their child will be held back. This is almost certainly not the case.

- A multi-cultural school will often have a diverse curriculum and a wide range of extra-curricular activities. For example, it could mark festivals and celebrations across the religious spectrum. It could provide Turkish lessons and classes in Caribbean drumming.
- EAL* students can often improve the learning opportunities of all students.
- Every school should have an Equal Opportunities Policy. It should be accessible upon request. However, such a document is worthless unless it is applied in the school, and you as a parent need to see it in action at first hand.
- I have found that in schools where there is a genuine multi-cultural mix, when there is no dominant race or culture in each class, students really do learn to be tolerant, because they have no other choice. In this situation, any child who is 'different' from the rest, for example, a middle class child in a school which

is predominantly working class, or a homosexual boy, is often just accepted as another one of the many minorities in the community. Children in this situation are used to difference. Every child will be 'different' to others at some time in their school career, so the better able the environment is to cope with that difference, the better time every child will have.

- In schools where there is a numerically dominant ethnic group, and very small minorities, it may be *a cause for concern* if your child is in the minority. However, you need not necessarily worry. If the school has a strong and effectively applied Equal Opportunities Policy, and therefore the minorities are well provided for, then sometimes the minority students can be in an advantageous position. If the minority is very small, then often other students do not recognise it, because they are not threatened by it.

- In a school with two predominant, potentially conflicting cultures, there is sometimes volatility. A school in this situation needs a strong Equal Opportunities Policy, rigorously applied, otherwise, *a cause for concern* may arise for parents.

- Undersubscribed schools often take more refugee students than other schools. LEAs will allocate students to a school which has places available. The transitional nature of the school intake becomes a concern. Refugee children are the most likely to move on to another school before their secondary schooling is complete. This creates instability in the learning environment.

Further Information
Ofsted
The 'Description of the School' will include details about the ethnic breakdown of the student cohort.
Prospectus
The prospectus may include an ethnic breakdown of the student cohort.
Open Evening/Visit
The school's Equal Opportunities Policy should be available on request.

To sum up:
It is unlikely that multi-culturalism in a school hinders progress. A school's multi-culturalism has the potential to benefit all students.

English as an Additional Language

EAL*/EMAG*

Some parents reading this book may themselves have English as an additional language. Some schools have a majority of students with English as an additional language, others have none. How schools manage students with English as a second language is an issue for all parents.

- A school which has any students with English as an additional language, EAL, should have a designated staff member with the responsibility for EAL/EMAG. A school with even a small minority of EAL students should have an EAL/EMAG department.

- The EAL/EMAG department will help students access the curriculum. A good department will promote multi-culturalism across the school.
- The EAL/EMAG department will be responsible for supporting any new students joining the school who do not have English as their first language. Parents without children in this position may think this irrelevant to them; but it is not. A school that has a strong induction programme for students for whom English is a second language, shows it values cultural diversity. Equally importantly, it indicates that the school is anxious to help new students access the curriculum quickly. This supports teachers and is to the benefit of everyone in the classroom.
- If your child does not speak English at home, it is important that you investigate the EAL/EMAG department. The quality of this department will strongly influence how well your child will be supported in their English literacy.
- If your first language is not English and you would benefit from school communications being translated, it is important that you find out whether this service is offered by the schools you are interested in.
- Parents whose children have English as their first language are often concerned that they will be held back if they attend a school with a lot of EAL students. I have rarely found this to be the case. If anything, the reverse often occurs. If there are non-English speaking students in the class, then the teacher is forced to be innovative about the way they present

ideas. Having non-English speaking students in the class often means there will be an EAL teacher or assistant present, which means that everyone has access to more support.

- Often students who speak two languages, one at home and one at school, are sophisticated learners and consequently help to establish a dynamic learning environment.

Further Information
Open Evening/Visit
Visit the EMAG/EAL department. Ask the student showing you round what happens to students at the school who do not speak English. The student should be clearly aware of a support system and have observed it in their lessons even if they do not have English language needs themselves.

Case Study
I once taught a Year 10 English class with two students who arrived at the school with no English at all. One was Chinese, the other from Ghana. By chance, both students were dedicated learners. The rest of the class watched with amazement as the two students, both girls, acquired English with rapidity and caught up with their peers. Some of the coasting students in the class, who found the subject easy, and were only performing at about 50% of their potential were put to shame when the two girls began achieving higher marks than them, and they raised their level of performance. The two girls did all the homework set with diligence and asked for more. The other students saw that doing homework well actually had the effect of improving

grades. Many students began to work harder as they saw at first hand the rewards of study. They could see what I had been telling them was true – if you did your homework and worked hard, you did get the grades you were capable of.

An EAL teacher came into my class once a week to support the girls. She helped with their homework, and produced extra support materials for them. Other students often asked for copies of these resources, which were, for example, simplified plots of the texts we were reading, to help them revise. The two girls would ask the other students if they did not understand things, which meant that the others had to understand things themselves before they could explain them.

The two girls, who had spoken English for only two years, achieved 'C' grades in their English GCSEs. It was also my best year for adding value at GCSE for the whole class. I am convinced that that success was in large part due to the presence of the two non-English speakers in my class.

To sum up:
Whether your child has English as their first or additional language, the quality of the EAL department and the languages spoken by the student cohort can impact positively on your child's school experience.

Friendship Groups

If your child's choice of secondary school was left entirely to them, they would almost always choose the school where their friends were going. However, there are things parents need to consider about friendship groups, before they decide which school is right for their child.

- If your child has friends at primary school who you feel are a negative influence, secondary transfer is a good opportunity for separating them. However, if your child has a tendency to always gravitate towards 'the naughty children' there will always be different 'naughty children' for them to hang out with in a new environment.

- Don't assume that just because a secondary school is the one that all the other parents from your primary school choose, that it is the right one for your child. Sometimes, these traditions are founded on something as unreliable as a school's reputation, which is often out of date, or simply upon geographical convenience.

- It is not a good idea to send your child to a particular secondary school simply so they can be with their friends. Many close friendships from primary school do not endure long into secondary school. There are too many new people and influences, and the children are going through too many changes for some friendships to be sustainable.

- However, if you are worried about your child's ability to make new friends, you might want to consider sending them to a school which the parents of well established friends are considering too. However, it is important to remember that your child or their friend might not gain a place in their first choice school. Even if they do, with the temptation of new peers, there is no guarantee that their friendship will last.

- It is worth pointing out that a good school will not allow students to sit in friendship groups in class that may jeopardise children's ability to learn. In a successful school, your child should not expect to sit with their friends in class or even share the same lessons.

- Schools should consult you and your child about friends coming up with them from primary school, when they are forming tutor groups*. They should take into consideration requests a parents might have for combinations of students to be separated.

- A good school will have a tutor group system, where a strong sense of group identity is established, so that your child will feel part of a community quickly, even if they have few peers from their primary school.

- If you are thinking of sending your child to a secondary school where few of her primary school friends are likely to attend, find out about the school's intake. If it is a school which has many feeder schools, then there should be no problem about your child settling in. If it is a school that takes from just a few feeder schools and your primary school is not one of them, then it might be more difficult for your child to integrate. However, I have often found in this situation, that the other children find new faces interesting, and a child from a different feeder school can get a lot of positive attention.

Further Information
LEA
If you are considering applying to schools because of friendship groups, make sure you are aware of the LEA*'s admissions* procedures, so you know what the likelihood is of your child and their friends attaining places at the same school.

Open Evening
Find out how tutor groups are made up, and whether parents are consulted. Find out what the school's transition* and induction processes are. Ask about the primary feeder schools.

Case Study
At School WH a student in a Year 7 tutor group was being bullied by classmates. It turned out that the bullies were from her old primary school. When challenged about their bullying, the students came out with a long list of provocations they felt they had received from this student in primary school, and although the student was no longer provoking them in the same way, and had attempted to turn over a new leaf, old attitudes seemed to have died hard. It was interesting that the mother of the student being bullied had been persuaded to choose the secondary school because of pressure put on her by her daughter who claimed to her mother that she wanted to be with all her friends. As it transpired, sadly, she considered the students who were bullying her to be her friends from primary school, although they did not consider that they had ever been friends with her. Here, there was obviously a convoluted history of difficult relationships from primary school that was hindering the

daughter at secondary school. The mother decided to move her daughter to a new secondary school in the hope that she could start afresh with new peers.

To sum up:
Primary school friendships often do not last in secondary schools and might not necessarily impact positively on learning.

Gifted and Talented

Parents are often most anxious about sending their child to a state school* if the child is gifted and talented*, or more able. There is a commonly held belief that state schools are not able adequately to stretch bright students, whereas independent schools* are. This is certainly not always the case, and it worthwhile investigating provision for gifted and talented students.

- All comprehensive schools* that are right for your child should have a programme for gifted and talented, or more able students.
- Schools with good programmes for able students run lots of extra initiatives to inspire and challenge; for example, university visits, extra-curricular clubs, and opportunities for extension work.
- Schools should have a clear idea of what a gifted and talented student should be able to achieve. They should be able to recognise academic excellence, and have a system under-stood by staff which enables more able

students to be identified and supported.

- Schools should have a system which specifically monitors the progress of gifted and talented students.
- There should be a member of staff with responsibility for more able students.
- Schools that get the best out of their gifted and talented students should have grades A* featuring frequently in their GCSE results and, if they have a 6th form, grades A at 'A' Level*.
- Schools should tailor a curriculum to the needs of gifted and talented students. For example, if a school sets* or streams* then top sets must be given an appropriately challenging curriculum. If a school has some mixed ability* subjects, then there must be an effective target setting system and appropriate extension work.
- A school with a good work ethos should celebrate high achieving students, and make them feel accepted by the whole student cohort. It is *a cause for concern* if a school has a culture where students feel embarrassed to be bright.
- If a school has lots of high achieving students, it does not necessarily mean it will be the best school for a highly able child. Sometimes, schools with a small cohort of gifted students are able to give them greater attention.
- Even if you do not consider your child to be more able, it is worth finding out about gifted and talented provision in schools which interest you. After all, it could be that your child turns out to be more able in later school life. Also, a school that celebrates the success of all

might be the one that is right for your child. It is also common that if more able students are challenged then the ethos of high standards rubs off on others too.

Further Information
Open Evening
In each subject area, ask to see examples of work by gifted and talented students. Ask to see the gifted and talented co-ordinator, or the member of staff who is responsible for more able students, and ask them about the programme on offer. Ask how the school identifies and monitors the progress of more able students.
Prospectus
A* grades should feature in the GCSE exam results and A grades in the 'A' Level results.
Visit
Ask to meet a more able student and ask them about their experiences.

To sum up:
A special programme for more able students, if properly applied, will benefit everyone in the school.

Head Teacher

The Head teacher of your child's school has a potentially huge impact on the quality of students' experiences.

- A good Head teacher has the respect of staff and students. The staff enjoy working for her, so there is not an abnormally large staff turnover. They also respect her, so they do not cut corners. Students see her as the ultimate sanction, but also trust her and are able to have productive relationships with her. She knows her students. This combination of skills is unusual and hard to find.

- A good Head teacher is visible and present. Some Head teachers shut themselves away in their office for so long they become afraid of students, and children do not know them. A good Head teacher is at the school gate, in the play ground, and in classrooms. They are omnipresent.

- A good Head teacher has positive relationships with parents, but is never held hostage to their whims. They consult with parents when appropriate, but have their own vision for the school.

- The Head teacher should involve parents appropriately in school decision making. For example, it is good practice to carry out an annual parents' survey and respond to its recommendations. However, the Head teacher has been appointed because they have the expertise to run the school and make decisions on behalf of the institution. A good Head teacher will steer a clear line between decisions which require parental consultation and those which should rely on her professional judgement.

- Good Head teachers are charismatic. When they talk, the listeners are inspired.

- A good Head teacher will be hands on. She should be there at the school production putting out the chairs if there is no one else to do it.

- A good Head teacher has a vision for the school, and talks in terms of what will happen in its future.
- Good Head teachers like children.
- If a Head teacher lacks key strengths, a strong leadership team can compensate. If the Head teacher, for example, is a strategist, and the Deputy Head* is an organiser, then this combination could be extremely successful.
- In a larger secondary school, it is often necessary for the Head teacher to be more of a figurehead, and to have strong Deputy Head teachers who do much of the day to day management. If the Deputies are of high calibre, then this situation can be more than satisfactory.
- Some Head teachers are often absent from the school. They may be on training courses, working with other schools or courting media attention. Again, this is not a problem so long as their presence is felt and they leave the management in the hands of capable Deputies.
- A Head teacher needs to be judged with regard to her school's context. If students come from backgrounds that negatively impact on academic progress; if the school is under funded; if the buildings are run down, and the Head still impacts positively, then arguably this is a far greater achievement than that of a Head who works in a school with supportive parents, a wealthy catchment* area, and an effective PTA*.

Further Information
Open Evening/Visit
Make sure you hear the Head teacher speak at open evening.

Ask the students who are showing you round about the Head. Your best answer is that she is 'strict but alright'. It does not matter if students dislike her so long as they perceive her as fair. Your worst answer is that they like her because she lets them get away with things. Ask the students where they see the Head teacher. Your best answer is 'everywhere.' A good answer is when they have done something very wrong, then they go to the Head teacher's office. An unsatisfactory answer is 'hardly ever.' However, if they mention a strict Deputy Head who is in charge of discipline, then this is acceptable.

Prospectus
The Head teacher will always write something in the prospectus, which will give you an indication of their calibre and philosophy.

School Profile
The tone of the profile, and its priorities, will give you an idea of the Head's vision for the school.

Case Study
School Y had a very good reputation. Essentially, this was because council housing had been demolished in its local area and private housing had replaced it. Consequently, the school's client group had changed and results had risen dramatically. The Head teacher took all the credit and was labelled a 'super Head' by the press. She was used by the government to promote their new initiatives

in education. She wrote columns for the press, and was frequently consulted by the media on educational issues. She was rarely seen in the school.

Were it not for the Deputy, the school would have lost the luck it had been dealt with its change of client group. The Deputy ran the school and was the de facto Head. She was both formidable and approachable. She was inspirational, organised and had good relationships with staff, students and parents, all of whom were loyal to her. She was unafraid of new initiatives which would raise the attainment of her students and enhance their experience of education. Because of the Deputy Head, it was a school I would have no hesitation sending my own child to.

To sum up:
Undoubtedly the quality of the Head teacher is an important factor to consider when choosing a school for your child. However, do not always take the apparent success of the Head at face value and consider the quality of the whole leadership team.

Learning Mentors

Some schools have learning mentors*. They do not teach classes. Learning mentors support students on a one to one or small group basis.

Learning mentors are specialist staff who work with students requiring motivation, support with organisation or who find relationships with people in authority complicated. Learning mentors act as a conduit between the student and the institution.

- In some schools, learning mentors focus on students who are at risk of exclusion*.
- Students who find it difficult to relate to the authority figure of a teacher can often relate better to a mentor.
- Parents who are fed up with always being contacted by the school with complaints about their child often find it easier to communicate with mentors.
- Students who do not work well in a classroom environment can often succeed with a mentor, who will sometimes take them out of the class and support them one to one.
- If a school has good mentors, it can have high success rates in keeping disaffected students in school without them being disruptive. These successes may not feature in Achievement and Assessment Tables*. In fact, if a school manages to retain students at risk of exclusion, this can often factor against them scoring highly in the tables. Even if a student at risk of exclusion manages to stay at school, they rarely achieve grades which match their potential, because they have spent so much of their school career underachieving.
- Even if your child is not a student who might be at risk of exclusion, it is worth investigating the quality of a school's learning mentors. There comes a time, albeit temporary, in most students' school life when they become disaffected to a degree. In this instance, it is often the figure of a learning mentor who maintains the link between the student and the school and keeps the student on track.

- The presence of learning mentors in a school invariably leads to a more nurturing and supportive atmosphere. Children and staff who do not meet with the mentor know that their peers do. The presence of learning mentors sends a message to the whole student and staff body that the school invests in support mechanisms.

Further Information
Open Evening
If the mentors are at the open evening, go and speak to them. Ask the learning mentors what the school success rate is at keeping students at risk of exclusion on course and in school.
Prospectus/Open Evening
Find out whether the school has mentors, and what types of students they work with.

Case Study
Michael was a very bright student, who had been in and out of trouble at school ever since he began his education. He had been permanently excluded from one primary school after a succession of violent tantrums, one of which culminated in chair throwing. It was by chance that he ended up at a secondary School L, where there were two outstanding learning mentors, one an ex primary school teacher, and one, an ex social worker. Michael was referred to the learning mentors after a term at the secondary school, having already received two fixed term exclusions for violent, over-reactive behaviour. Very quickly, the learning mentors worked out a programme with Michael

which reduced his excesses and, although he was by no means a star pupil, he managed to stay at school. Because he was bright, in Year 10, he actually started to make significant progress in certain subjects, and at the end of the year, he won the school's prize for most improved pupil. He did not feature in the school's league table statistics, because he did not get five or more A*–C GCSE grades, and did not meet his potential. However, the huge achievement was that he stayed at school. After working in a supermarket for a year after leaving school, he went to college and did a vocational course in catering. He is now a chef.

To sum up:
Learning mentors can enrich the fabric of a school, and they might be the people who have a direct positive impact on your child.

Parents

Successful schools often have children who receive strong support for learning from parents. In fact studies[2] have suggested that the quality of parental support could be the single most important factor in determining how well a child does at school. Finding out about the parent cohort at a school and investigating a school's relationship with its parent

---

[2] Macbeth, A., (1988) 'Research about Parents in Education', In S. Brown and R. Wake, (Eds), 'Education in Transition; What Role for Research?', The S.C.R.E., Edinburgh.

group is therefore a key element in deciding upon the right school for your child.

- If a school has an active Parent Teachers Association, PTA*, the likelihood is that it has a parent body that supports learning.
- It is important to look carefully at what the school does for parents, as well as what the parent body does for the school. A school which tries hard to engage parents, even though parents may be difficult to engage, is better than a school that does not try at all.
- A successful school involves parents in children's learning. For example, they might have parents helping at a school production, or parents reading with students.
- Parents should be made welcome at the school. They should be greeted hospitably and warmly by reception, and the school should facilitate all communication with parents, not hinder it.
- It should be made very clear by the school whom parents should contact about issues concerning their children.
- A school with a strong pastoral* system usually has good communications with parents. Tutors* are accessible and know their students well. The school contacts parents with good news as well as bad. The school contacts parents when they can help, not when it is too late.
- Schools which successfully communicate with parents are more likely to be right for your child. A school should have ways of having a

regular dialogue with parents. Usually, schools will have a system where each student has a journal* to record homework, important dates and information; and which parents and tutors sign every week. If the use of this journal is not enforced by the school, then the system is useless.

- Schools should make all appropriate publications accessible to parents. The School Profile*, the prospectus, and the newsletter should all be parent friendly.

- Schools which want to communicate with all of their parents and not just a select few will make sure that key communications are appropriately translated.

- A school will usually have some sort of newsletter which it sends out to parents, keeping them up to date. If this publication is working, it should be informative, celebrate success, be published regularly and actually be read by parents.

- Schools should have means of regularly informing parents about their child's performance. Legally, a school has to produce a report for each child at least once a year. Some schools also give every parent an end of term breakdown of levels or grades. In others, teachers record progress in the students' journals. If communications are working successfully, a parent should be able to find out, with little difficulty, what level their child is working at in each subject at any time.

- Parents should be invited to school at least once a year for a parents' evening* or an

Academic Review* day to discuss their child's progress.

- Schools should have a schedule of parents' events. These should not be limited to parents' evenings. Successful schools could hold revision evenings, options' evenings or curriculum evenings. Schools should be facilitating parental involvement at all the key points of your child's career.
- All extended schools* are required to offer a full programme for parents, which includes parenting support.
- Schools that want to listen to their parents' views often carry out parent surveys.
- Some Head teachers are better at and more interested in communicating with parents than others. A good Head teacher works hard to involve and inform parents.
- Remember that a Head teacher is not at the beck and call of parents. Although the notion of 'parent choice' is very popular at the time of writing, the Head teacher is a highly qualified professional who knows their own mind, not simply that of their parent body. As well as listening to parents, a Head teacher sometimes needs to stand up to them. Not all parents will have the good of the school at the top of their agenda, and a Head teacher must not be intimidated by parents or respond to their every whim.

Further Information
Extra-curricular
Contact the school and ask about extra-curricular*

events, such as the school production. If possible attend a school's production before you decide whether to send your child there. You will get to observe the parental cohort in the audience, and you can chat to the parents who are usually involved providing the refreshments.

Informal Visit

Pop into the school to pick up the prospectus. See how the reception staff treat you as prospective parents, whether they are warm and welcoming, or indifferent.

Open Evening

Find out if the school has a parental survey and if so what they have learned from it. Have any actions been taken as a result of the survey findings? Ask about their reporting cycle.

PTA

It is helpful to talk to parents of children who attend the school you are considering. One way of doing this is to contact the school and see if there are any events coming up that are organised by the PTA, for example, a school fete, or other fund raising event. If there is, get tickets and go. Then, you can get a feel for the type of parents involved, and whether you would fit in with them. You can also ask them informally about the school, and what their endorsements or reservations are.

School Profile

The section 'How are we working with parents and the community' will give you an idea of the school's relationship with its parent cohort.

School Publications

Contact the school and ask for any recent back copies of their communications with parents:

letters, examination time tables etc. This will give you an idea about how hard the school works to involve its parents, and also give you a taste of how the Head teacher addresses her parents.

It is a good idea to ask the school for the most recent copy of their newsletter and two or three back copies. See how often the newsletter comes out, see if the school celebrates its success, and see if there is any evidence from the newsletter of parents actually reading it, for example, comments from parents etc.

Visit

Ask the student showing you round about their journal or day book. Find out whether their parents and tutors regularly sign it.

To sum up:
The nature of a school's relationship and communication with parents can have a significant impact on the school's success.

Siblings

The presence of siblings can give you an indication of a school's popularity.

- If parents send younger siblings to the same school as older brothers and sisters, it would suggest that they are satisfied with the provision.
- However, it is important to note that parents might send their younger children to the same school because of convenience rather than

active choice.

- If younger siblings attend the school, then it is more likely to have a family atmosphere, and a sense of its own history.
- If younger siblings attend the school, then it is more likely that it fosters a sense of loyalty among its student cohort.
- It is *a cause for concern* if a school attracts less able brothers and sisters, with the higher achievers going elsewhere.

Further Information
Open Evening/Visit
Ask what proportion of parents send their younger children to the school. Ask the student showing you round how many of his/her friends have brothers or sisters at the school.

To sum up:
If parents are happy with a school, it is likely they will send their second child after the first.

Special Educational Needs

SEN*

Parents of children with special educational needs should look for a school with a strong special needs department. However, the quality of special needs provision affects all students in a school.

Every school has students with special needs. Much depends on how they are motivated and supported.

- Some children have a statement of special needs. This means they have particular needs and a statement has been drawn up to define the extra support they are entitled to. The LEA* is obliged to fund the support, and the school must deliver the statement.
- Statemented students are normally given the secondary school of their choice.
- Most children with special needs do not qualify for a statement. The government does not provide extra money to the school for these students and they are largely dependent upon the school's special needs department.
- The right school for your child is likely to have a strong special needs department, regardless of whether your child has special needs or not. The better SEN students access to the curriculum, the better the standards of student motivation and behaviour across the school will be.
- An effective special needs department provides extra support and sanctuary for students with a wide array of learning, behaviour and social difficulties. It has a high profile and its staff are respected by all students. In this way, all students are educated to be tolerant of those with additional needs.
- Although most students are not diagnosed as having special needs, all students will have a 'special need' at some point in their school career. For example, they may be very confident and academic, but suffer a bereavement which means they need counselling. They may have always done well in every subject, but

suddenly find a block in a particular area. Indeed, being gifted and talented* is commonly included within a school's definition of 'special needs'. If a school has a strong special needs department, then it provides access to all students who need its support. Parents sometimes make the mistake of thinking their children will never need additional support, when this is rarely the case.

- Schools' Achievement and Assessment Tables* include measures of the percentage of Year 11* students who have attained five or more grade A*–C grades. It is important to recognise, however, that your child might not be in that ability range. A school with a good special needs department will have a high success rate in helping students to attain at least one A*–G grade. Most parents hope their children will be in the A*–C category. However, for all sorts of reasons, they might not end up in there, and a parent needs to know that their child will receive support whatever their likely level of achievement.

- A school with a strong special needs department is inclusive, involving all students whatever their gender, culture and aptitude. A school with a weak special needs department may not have an inclusive ethos. In this case the school might not value or acknowledge the range of abilities its students possess.

- When considering the issue of special needs, parents must decide what they want from a school. Those who want their children to appreciate the inclusion in society of students with a variety of disabilities and needs should find a school with a good special needs department.

- Parents of children without special needs are often wary of schools with a large special needs cohort. Their concern should not be the size of the cohort, but how it is managed. If the school has a strong special needs department, students will be supported so that they do not hold up the progress of others. Indeed, an effective SEN department will enhance the progress of all. If a school does not have a strong special needs department, then students with special needs are more likely to hinder others' progress in the classroom.

- Special needs departments are staffed by specialist teachers and teaching assistants*. If a school has strong teaching assistants, this can benefit all students, not just those with special needs. In lessons, a good classroom assistant is another resource to help them learn.

- A strong special needs department will help all teachers with their workload. It will help with classroom resources and methods of support for special needs students. This help will mean that all students get on better in the classroom.

- If your child has special needs, it important you find out what expertise exists in the special needs department. For example, if they suffer from dyspraxia*, it would be helpful to know whether there is a dyspraxia specialist in the department, and how the school has dealt historically with students with dyspraxia.

- If your child has special needs, it is important to

ascertain how well resourced the special needs department is, in terms of staffing ratios and facilities.

- If your child has special needs, it is important to find out how students with special needs are taught. For example, are they withdrawn from classes in some subject areas, or are they supported in the class.

- If your child has issues in literacy, you must see what programme the school provides to help students improve their reading in Year 7*. For example, some schools have an intensive reading programme to speed up students' literacy development and help them access the curriculum.

- Special needs is a political issue. Sometimes good schools do not advertise their special needs department, because they do not want to attract too high a number of special needs students. Special needs students might impact negatively on a school's Achievement and Assessment Tables rating.

- Grammar schools* are likely to have small special needs departments. However, special needs exist in all student cohorts, so a good selective school should still take special needs seriously.

Further Information
Open Evening
If your child has special needs, you must meet the SEN Co-ordinator at open evening, and ask how your child's needs would be catered for. It is very important that you feel that you could work effec-

tively with this person.

Primary School

If your child has special needs, speak to the responsible teacher at their primary school. They will have contact with secondary school special needs departments and will be able to tell you about their quality.

Prospectus

The school prospectus should have a section on special needs provision. If it does not, it might be that the school is denying that the issue exists, or overlooking it. This would be *a cause for concern*.

The school prospectus will include exam results. In order to ascertain the strength of the special needs department you need to look at the percentages that relate to A*–Gs, and not just A*–Cs.

Visit

When visiting the school in working hours, make sure you locate the special needs department and assess how welcoming and productive the environment feels.

Case Study

School F had a strong special needs department. At this school, Wendy was top of all her classes. She had never been referred to the special needs department in her school life. When she was in Year 10, her mother died. It was a critical time in Wendy's academic career. Her father could not cope, and Wendy's achievement suffered. She was referred to the special needs department. The department did her laundry for her because her father, in his grief, had lost any interest in personal hygiene. Wendy had exam anxiety and the special needs department worked through the panic attacks with her. After school Wendy helped students in the SEN department with their homework. This helped her regain her confidence, and made her more able to take on an adult role at home. She did not feel like doing the revision she needed to at home, and explaining concepts to other students when helping them with their homework worked as effective revision for her. When GCSE results were published Wendy underachieved in only one subject area.

To sum up:
It is important to research a school's special needs department, regardless of whether your child officially has special needs or not. A good special needs department impacts positively upon all students in a school.

Teaching Staff

The quality of teaching staff is a key contributor in whether your child will be successful at school. Your child will benefit from a team of stable staff, who have a good record of adding value to students' achievements.

- The fewer staff vacancies at a school, the better. At the time of writing, there remain lots of areas in the country with teacher shortages, particularly in Maths and Science. If a school finds it difficult to recruit, this is *a cause for concern*.

- Teaching provided by supply* staff is problematic. Students notoriously misbehave or at least do little work when faced with a supply teacher. Learning is certainly not a priority. Even the most responsible of students tends to avoid work, if taught by a supply teacher.
- Schools often use long term supply staff in hard to fill vacancies. This is not ideal for students. Even if the supply teacher is good, they are not part of the institution, they are new to its systems, they have no obligation to stay. They might be unfamiliar with the exam syllabus the students are studying. They might not be prepared to attend parents evenings or mark students' work.
- Unfortunately there are lots of weak supply teachers. Sometimes, teachers do supply work because they cannot get a permanent job. If your child is taught by a number of weak long term supply teachers, this is *a cause for concern*.
- It is not satisfactory for students to be taught by a series of short term supply teachers. This sometimes happens when a reliable long term supply teacher cannot be found. In this scenario, there is no continuity of learning; students' work might be lost; work will often be set by other teachers who do not know where the students are in the curriculum; homework might not be set; marking might not be completed.
- Students learn best if their learning environment is stable. Teachers raise achievement most effectively if they are familiar with a child's particular learning needs, strengths and

weaknesses. Any circumstance which results in a high turnover of teachers for your child is *a cause for concern*.

- Students learn better in a secure environment. Constant turnover of staff creates insecurity.

- It is *a cause for concern*, if there is a high staff turnover, and staff are making sideways moves, going for demotions, or getting out of teaching altogether. This pattern suggests that there is something seriously wrong at the school on a fundamental level.

- If students are working in an environment where high staff turnover is the norm, they can get into the habit of testing the teacher, to see if the teacher can 'hack it'. They spend more time pushing new teachers to their limits, than concentrating on learning.

- A school where staff never leave might not be the right place either. A lively innovative atmosphere is one where learning flourishes. If staff are bored, cynical, or complacent, then this will not encourage progress in the students.

- A successful school trains up its teachers to be ambitious for the students and for themselves. A healthy school has some teacher turnover, perhaps about 5–10% per year, with the staff leaving going on to promotion.

- It is quite usual for a number of staff to leave when a new Head takes up post. This is not necessarily a bad thing. If the Head has new ideas and some staff are not ready to embrace these, then it is best if they move on. Also, if the Head is good, she will attract new staff who add vitality to the school. There is also a pattern that staff will stay with a new Head for two or three years and then decide to move on. This again, is not necessarily a bad thing. It can often mean that the Head is starting to kick things into shape and that some staff are not up to it. What is *a cause for concern*, however, is if the Head has been there for five or six years and the staff turnover is still consistently high. This means that the Head has failed to establish a good relationship with her staff, and if the staff are not content, nor will the students be.

• At the time of writing, because of teacher shortages in subjects like Maths and Science, it is common to find non-specialists teaching classes. This is not necessarily a cause for concern up to and including Key Stage 3. Their ability to teach and their knowledge of how to pass an exam are actually going to have a higher impact on your child than graduate level knowledge. If a member of staff cannot teach, then it does not matter how much they know. If they have no idea of the exam requirements then no amount of subject knowledge is going to help them. A teacher who is inspirational, hard working and very familiar with the exam system is a good bet for your child. A teacher who has all these things, and an expansive subject knowledge is even better, particularly for students who are gifted and talented*.

• Subject expertise is essential at Key Stage 4 and in post 16 teaching.

• It is the policy of some schools to list the qualifications and place of study of their staff, particularly if some of them attended Oxbridge. Again, if the staff are not proficient in teaching skills, it does not matter from where they got their degree. It is worth noting that if someone has never found it hard to learn, they often find it hard to teach, because they do not understand the obstacles that others have to learning. Sometimes, the best teachers are the ones who understand how difficult a subject can be, not how easy.

- A 'good' teacher is essentially one who adds value*. A child in their class has potential and the teacher enables the child to meet that potential, or even better, exceed expectations.

- Students learn well if they have a positive working relationship with a teacher. However, students' favourite teachers are not necessarily the most effective ones. A favourite among students for example, might entertain with jokes but not stick to the syllabus. What you as a parent are looking out for is a school where teachers inspire respect.

- Very few secondary schools will have a staff where every teacher is 'good'. In fact, even in successful schools, there is usually at least one teacher who is seen as notoriously ineffective by the students. However, parents must be assured that the majority of teachers are good enough and that the school is taking necessary steps to make sure students are not hindered by weak teaching.

- It is *a cause for concern* if your child has a special interest, for example, music, where the department is likely to be small, and the teacher is weak.

- It is *a cause for concern* if the majority of a core* department's teachers are weak.

- A large, strong department may carry one weak teacher and protect students against their potential effects. A strong Head of Department* can oversee weak teachers, for example, to maintain good behaviour among the students. A strong department will plan and work collaboratively and have very well formulated, centralised units of work* which help all teachers to teach well. A Head of Department with a very good knowledge of the subject's exam, can ensure all colleagues are able to pass on examination requirements.

- Because there will always be weaker teachers in every school, and because you cannot guarantee that your child will never encounter one, it is vital to find out whether a school department or faculty is strong enough to carry a weaker staff member.

- In some departments, the Head of Department takes all of the high sets themselves and leaves the other classes for her colleagues. This might not be a good thing because it is actually much harder to add value to lower ability students' performance than to that of higher ability students. Sometimes, weaker teachers have a very good subject knowledge, but poor classroom management skills. They therefore might be better suited to high ability and better motivated classes who behave better and would benefit from more extensive subject knowledge.

- A department that allocates its weaker teachers entirely to low ability groups shows that it only values high achieving students.
- There is no guarantee that particular teachers, good or bad, will be at the school throughout your child's career there. It is important to establish the general staff turnover situation, rather than glean information about particular individuals.

Further Information
National Media/TES
When you are considering schools, buy the TES* or access it on-line (www.tes.co.uk) and see if there are regular vacancies at your preferred school – this will give you some idea if there is a high staff turnover. Remember though that the bigger the school, the larger the number of teachers one might expect to see coming and going.

Open Evening
Make sure you talk to the heads of all core departments, English, Maths and Science, and ask them about their value added and how they maintain standards. Ask them how long they have been at the school. Ask other Heads of Department about how long the teachers have been in their department and whether they have any vacancies, or long term supply teachers.

Ask any teachers about staff turnover in the school. Ask how many teachers left last term and the term before. If seems to be over 20% of the staff, then this is *a cause for concern*.

Visit
Ask the student showing you round whether there

are any teachers who allow students to mess about in class. If they say one or two, then that is not a serious worry. If they list three or more staff, then that is *a cause for concern*.

Ask the student if there are always lots of new teachers at the school, or whether most have been there for some time.

Case Study
At School H, a new Head teacher took over and her style was very different to her predecessor's. The school was not doing well in the Achievement and Assessment Tables, and the new Head's remit was to bring in change and improve results. Because of her change in style, about a third of the staff left within a year of her arriving at the school. The Head teacher, in advertising for new staff made a virtue of her newness and the idea of a fresh start. She recruited good staff who were enthusiastic to move the school forward. However, it soon became apparent that the Head teacher was not effective at managing people, so the new arrivals also started thinking about moving on. For another year or so, the Head teacher was still able to recruit, because she could make a virtue out of being new, but after having been at the school for three years, replacement staff became thin on the ground. Within these three years, 75% of the teaching staff had left. Students had little continuity of teaching, long term supply teachers were common, and results continued to stagnate. It was only when the Head teacher left and another was recruited that staff retention issues were successfully addressed and results began to improve.

To sum up:
Your child needs consistency. The right school for them will be a place where most staff stay and a small proportion regularly move on for promotion. It does not matter how knowledgeable a teacher is if they cannot effectively impart that knowledge to their students through strong classroom management skills.

'Beyond the Classroom'

Destinations

It is worth finding out where students go when they leave a school. This will tell you what kind of aspirations the school is instilling in its students and what kind of careers the school is preparing them for.

- A school with a 6th form*, where most students go on to university, is clearly an academic institution. Check university take up levels if your child is likely to be academic.
- A school which has a variety of destinations for students, with or without a 6th form, some going on to FE* or HE*, taking academic and vocational* subjects at college, students going on to employment, some beginning apprenticeships, shows that the institution celebrates diversity, and encourages students of all abilities and aptitudes to flourish.
- A school where very few students go on to FE or HE suggests an institution that is not academic, and it could suggest a school which has failed to foster ambition or a love of learning. A school where most students go on to work related courses suggests a vocational* bias. However, this could be the right school for your child, if you think that they are more likely to succeed in an FE or HE vocational course.
- Some students will not go on to FE or HE. It is important to find out what record your chosen school has in moving students straight into

employment. If over 5% of leavers are unemployed, then that is *a cause for concern*.

- A school where most of the students who do go on to FE or HE go to the same colleges and institutions suggests that clear progression routes have been established. This might be the right school for your child, if you feel they would lack confidence about going on to further or higher education, as they would be accompanied by students they knew following the same path. However, it could also be that the school has not fostered a sense of ambition in its students, and has given them rather provincial aspirations. It is *a cause for concern* if students just go to the local FE or HE institution, because they have not been given the confidence or information about the other options.

- A school should have careers' advice which helps students to choose the FE, HE or employment route which suits them best. The school should enable students to choose the right courses. Competition for students is keen in both the FE and HE sectors. It is important that schools provide their students with high quality objective advice to assist them in making informed decisions.

- It is important to look at the careers and the FE and HE subjects students are choosing. If some subject areas are poorly represented, this suggests that those school departments are not fostering enthusiasm and aspiration in students.

- A preponderance of destinations in one

subject, for example, PE, BTECs* in Leisure and Tourism, jobs in Leisure Centres, signings for football teams, and PE 'A' Levels*, shows that the school is strong in that curriculum area. A specialist* school should have students pursuing the specialism at FE and HE.

Further Information
Prospectus
A school prospectus should carry a list of students' destinations for the previous year.
Open Evening
Talk to the careers* adviser. Speak to some Year 11 students, or 6th formers. Ask them about their aspirations. Ask them which FE or HE institutions ex-students attend. Speak to a member of senior management* about the destinations of students. Ask to speak to the current Head of Year 11 or the Head of 6th form. Ask them to tell you about the usual destinations of students.
Visit/Open Evening
If students are showing you round, ask them if they have older brothers and sisters who went to the school, who have now left. Ask what these siblings went on to do.

Many schools will have a board displaying HE destinations. This may seem traditional but it shows the school takes a pride in where its students move on to after leaving.

Case Study
School SH was an effective school in many ways, but it had failed to foster in its students a sense of aspiration and ambition that went beyond the

constraints of their community. The school was in the suburbs of a large city. The students rarely travelled into the city centre, or used any amenities outside a 5 mile radius of the school and home. The school recruited very few students from outside its immediate locality. However it was an improving institution and students were beginning to achieve increasingly highly.

James was a particularly bright boy, who was benefiting from the school's improvement. He left school in Year 11 with ten GCSEs, all As or Bs, achievement which was an accurate reflection of his ability.

There was no 6th form at the school, and most of the school's students went to the nearest FE college, although it was by no means the best. James took three 'A' Levels, and was doing very well in all of them. Two of them were not his first choices, but the institution did not offer the subjects he had originally wanted to do. James was predicted 'A' grades in his 'A' Levels, and decided he wanted to do a Media degree. The university in the city did have a Media course, but it did not have a good reputation. The entry requirement was 3 'C's at 'A' Level. However, because of the limited aspirations of James' peers, it never occurred to him to go anywhere else. His parents were proud he was going to university, and were not informed enough to know that there were other courses that might have been better.

James got the required grades and went to study Media at the city's university. He is doing very well. However, in the competitive media workplace, he will not have the head start of having been on a more prestigious course at a higher profile university. Although he went to an improving school, its inability to challenge provincial horizons hampered James' chances of future success.

To sum up:
It is worth investigating students' destinations at the school you are considering, to see what the long term future might hold for your child if they go there.

Extra-curricular Activities

The extra-curricular* activities a school provides can make or break whether a student enjoys their time there.

- At the time of writing, the government intends to make all schools extended schools* by 2010. Extended schools have to provide a programme of extra-curricular activities between 8.00am and 6.00pm. If a school is only offering a few extra-curricular activities then this is *a cause for concern*.
- Schools should provide some additional activities which are directly related to improving performance, for example revision sessions at Key Stage 3* and GCSE*.
- Schools that offer a variety of more creative extra activities, for example, a magazine club, a netball club, a debating club, indicate that they have a committed and enthusiastic staff. It is nearly always the case that teachers do these

kinds of extra-curricular activities in their own time, so their existence demonstrates a level of dedication and reveals a staff who enjoy spending time with young people.

- The right school for your child should provide extra activities for students with a variety of needs. There should be extra-curricular provision for gifted and talented* students, and those with special educational needs.* Learning mentors* might run a lunchtime games' club, it could be that this club is for students who feel they don't fit in anywhere else. If the special needs department runs a homework club, it will probably focus on those students who have difficulty with homework.

- It is a good sign if a variety of departments provide extra-curricular activities. If it is just the PE department, then the school is providing only a basic expectation. If, however, clubs are run by most departments, there is obviously a whole school ethos of extending learning.

- Classroom teaching must increasingly focus on preparing students for exams. However, it is often more creative activities, not directly related to the curriculum, which lead to students feeling more involved and committed. A school that provides activities that are not just strictly academic shows that it values educating the whole child.

- Extra-curricular activities often help form friendship groups. They assist students in making connections with others beyond their tutor group*, year group, or immediate peer group. A parent might look for a school with strong extra-curricular provision, if they feel their child finds it difficult to form friendships. If a child chooses the right extra-curricular club, they could find like minded peers and make friends. For example, if a student was gifted and talented it is worth finding out what clubs are provided for the more able students.

- There are some subject areas where extra-curricular provision is essential, for example PE, Music, and Drama.

- If your child has a particular passion for a subject such as Drama, then the quality of extra-curricular provision could define their secondary school career. A student who loves writing could flourish at school if they were part of a successful school newspaper.

- In most schools, lunchtimes and the end of the day are when incidents of poor behaviour tend to occur. A parent who is worried about their child getting involved in such incidents should look for a school which has extra-curricular provision to attract them during these key times.

- If a school allows its students to go off site at lunchtime, and you would rather they stayed at school then find out what lunchtime activities take place.

- If you are considering sending your child to a specialist* school there should be extra-curricular activities in the specialism.

- Some schools recruit outside providers to deliver extra-curricular activities, for example, a football club. Such organisations can support students who find relationships difficult with the school staff.

- The right school for your child will have lots of events that enrich the core curriculum. For example, the English department might have visiting poets; the Citizenship department might have presenters from the emergency services; the Drama department might get in productions from theatre companies. Exposure from a variety of outside sources and opinions provides students with a richer experience of learning. A school that has a variety of provision within its school day is also a confident school. It trusts its students to behave well with adults other than their teachers.

- In almost all cases, extra-curricular provision, trips, and the involvement of outside providers in curriculum enhancement are good things. However, a school should have systems in place for making sure that students' participation is balanced. It is counter productive, for example, if a student does nothing but participate in Drama productions at the expense of their homework. It is no good if a student is a brilliantly disciplined football player, but never behaves in class. Some schools do not let Year 11 or 13 students participate in school productions in their last year of study to ensure they do not jeopardise their chances of exam success. Some schools will ban students from representing the school in sport, if they consistently disrupt in class. You should look for these checks and balances to ensure your child gets the most from their education.

School Trips

- The right school for your child will provide a range of learning experiences that go beyond the classroom. Every child, no matter what their learning style will benefit from a variety of activities. It is therefore important to find out what trips are provided in all year groups not just Year 7.
- If a school does not provide any trips then that is *a cause for concern*.
- Schools have different attitudes to trips and their benefits. Some schools, for example, send each year group off to a theme park for the day in the summer. They justify this by saying that education is about rewards and relationships. Some schools, however, only run trips that they believe link directly with the curriculum.
- Trips are hard work for staff. They require a lot of paperwork. If staff go on trips out of school hours, they do not get paid extra, or get time in lieu. Schools that run trips then, have staff who are committed and enthusiastic enough to give extra effort and time.
- On trips, the school is always on show. Schools that run a lot of trips are confident about the ability of their students to present themselves well in public.
- If you ask a teenager or adult what they enjoyed most at school, they often say it was the trips. Trips can be excellent for developing relationships among students. Trips and extra-curricular provision are often spaces where staff and students form stronger bonds; rela-

tionships which make students feel more secure at their school and work harder for their teachers.

- It is often children's fear, innate conservatism and provincialism that hinder their academic achievement. They are afraid of the unfamiliar. They do not want to try new things. They often lack exposure to ideas that might help them improve their learning. A school that provides opportunities beyond the curriculum and the school gate breaks down these barriers to teaching, learning and social development.
- A school that regularly offers expensive trips should have a support fund so that all students can access opportunities.

School Productions

It is worthwhile attending a school's productions if you are interested in it for your child.

- If the production is well attended, that shows you that the school has active parental support.
- The Parent Teacher Association* will often organise refreshments. Talk to its representatives over coffee.
- Usually, school students will attend the production, and you need to assess their behaviour and discipline as audience members. Look for students who are there to listen and not disrupt, and who want to give a good impression of their school. Teachers should be on hand to keep the audience in order as well

as to supervise the production. It is *a cause for concern* if students are left to disrupt in the audience without intervention.

- If there are a number of teachers involved in the production, and staff as members of the audience, then that is a sign of a committed staff.

- Look for a school where departments clearly work together. Good props, music, costumes and acting shows a school where there is collaboration between staff.

- It is important that the event is well managed. Staff should be at the door welcoming guests and keeping students in control. It is a good sign if the Head teacher is present. On the last night, effusive speeches from the Head thanking teachers and students involved show a school which has a strong sense of community. If the Head teacher is absent, and there are very few staff in attendance, that could indicate a school where staff will not go that extra mile, and it may be that the Head teacher is not committed to all areas of the curriculum.

- If the tickets sell out quickly, this indicates that the students and parents are involved and care about their school.

- If the school holds no productions, this is *a cause for concern*.

- If a rogue element turns up in the audience, students there to cause disruption, then that is *a cause for concern*. A similar element may be present in the school during lesson time.

- If your child is keen on Drama, Music or Art, then the quality of the production is important.

- The choice of production tells you something about the school. Some schools do a major musical every year. This tells you that the Arts departments work together. It may be important to some parents that school productions reflect the cultural diversity of their intake. Some schools take on serious pieces of drama, which reveals that the Drama department is ambitious and wishes to stretch students intellectually.
- Do not be too judgemental about the quality of the actual singing or acting. If there are one or two outstanding performers, it could be that the school is lucky to have them in their cohort. If the students are involved, well rehearsed and enthusiastic these are good signs. Try to be aware how much the fondness of parenthood can create a gloss on the production for the audience.
- If the production is under-rehearsed and badly acted this reflects on the commitment and ability of the Drama and/or Music department(s).
- Some school productions are outstanding. This shows that the Arts are strong in the school. It can also tell you something about the school's sense of scale. For example, some schools can stage a musical with a quality of staging, acting and music that is not very short of a professional production. This indicates that the school has ambition and a sense of its wider audience.
- A Performing Arts College should put on excellent productions.

School Concerts

Similar principles apply to school concerts as dramatic productions.

- The choice of content is often telling. For example, a school could make a particular effort to reflect the multi-cultural nature of its community through its choice of music.
- A staff choir reveals commitment and loyalty to the school.
- Sometimes a school can pay musicians or performers to bolster the performance. This can deceive the audience as to the quality of the school's Music or Drama departments. It is important to ask a member of staff on duty if any non-school staff took part.
- If the school puts on no concerts then this is *a cause for concern*.
- A Performing Arts College should put on excellent concerts.

Further Information
Open Evening
Ask each department what extra-curricular activities they carry out and how regularly these things happen. Ask what their recent concerts and productions have been. Look out for displays of recent productions, trips and extra-curricular events. Make sure you check the dates.
School Productions
Contact the school and ask for details of the next school concert or school production so you can attend.

School Publications
Contact the school and ask for a copy of school publications which feature school trips, for example, a calendar of events, a school year book, school newsletters.

School Profile
The section 'What activities are available to pupils?' gives you information about extra-curricular activities.

Visit
Ask the student showing you round whether they take part in any extra-curricular activities, and whether most students do.

Case Study
School C had a regular programme of ambitious Music and Drama productions. The plays and music chosen were often quite highbrow. However, the Heads of Drama and Music, who undoubtedly worked very well together, were not really interested in the whole cohort of students. They put a lot of time into students who were gifted in their subject areas, but largely neglected the others. To put on performances, they used their best students, ex students, and their musician and actor friends. So, although the productions were impressive, they did not represent the interests and talents of school students.

To sum up:
Extra-curricular activities can be the key to whether your child enjoys school or not.

A strong programme of activities shows the school values the whole child.

A school concert or production can give you a

revealing insight into what the school might be like on a day to day basis.

Transition and Induction

Transition* is the name given to the phase of education which covers movement between primary and secondary school. It is common for there to be a 'dip' in students' achievement at the transition stage. For example, a student can commonly end up at the end of Year 7* with lower National Curriculum levels than they achieved at the end of Year 6.

Induction is the process of settling a Year 7 student into their secondary school. The quality of the experience a young person receives in their first few days at a new school can impact on their subsequent career.

Parents will often say that a child, who was successful at primary school, inexplicably begins to fail at secondary school. Therefore, the right secondary school for your child will offer transition and induction processes that seek to counter potential dips in performance.

- Many secondary schools will send someone, often the prospective Head of Year 7, to primary schools, to visit Year 6 students who have been allocated a place at their school. This can have a positive effect, as it gives the students a chance to ask questions in an environment that feels secure.
- Most secondary schools interview the Year 6

students who have been allocated a place, to gather details, and get to know the child. Often parents are invited or requested to be present at the interview. This can help the student feel secure and valued, and shows that the school is taking children's individual needs into consideration.

- Schools which liaise regularly with local primaries, for example, working on joint lesson provision, sharing facilities and holding joint functions, have a better track record in avoiding the Year 7 dip, because they are more familiar with the primary school context from which their students come.

- Schools which give Year 6 students work to do over the summer holidays to prepare them for Year 7 mean business. It is an even better sign if the school then acknowledges the work properly at the start of the new academic year, and incorporates it into the students' new studies.

- Schools which take samples of Year 6 students' work and use them to assess the students' starting point in Year 7 are serious about countering the Year 7 'dip'.

- Secondary schools often have an induction taster day for the students allocated a place in Year 7. This can help reduce the new students' anxiety about the unknown.

- If a school organises an induction taster day, it should set a precedent by running smoothly. The day should be set up in such a way that Year 6 students end it motivated, reassured, and secure. It is a good sign if the Year 6 students have been introduced to the Head teacher, and other key members of staff on the induction day.

- Secondary schools should have a very organised programme for the new students' arrival on their first day, and parents should be told about it well in advance. Common practice is for the Year 7 students to arrive in school without the other year groups, so that they get used to the building without being overwhelmed by older students. So, for example, Year 7 might begin the first day of term in the morning, and the rest of the school join them in the afternoon.

- Secondary schools should be clear about the equipment they want the students to bring, so that every family has the chance to get their child prepared. A list should be published well in advance of the student beginning in Year 7.

- The school will have someone who is in charge of the Year 7 group, either a Head of Year or House*. These members of staff should be introduced to the Year 6 students in advance of their arrival at the school, either through a primary school visit, or an induction taster day.

- Often parents feel more anxious about transition than their children, and this parental anxiety feeds into the Year 7 'dip'. Consequently, the right school for your child should respond to the anxieties of parents. Ideally, every parent should have met a member of staff before their child begins at the school. Information about all aspects of transition should be clear and sent in good time, to minimise potential parental anxiety. A school might invite parents in for refreshments on the taster day to make it easier for them to leave their child. Sometimes schools make sure there is PTA* contact with new parents prior to their child's arrival, so established parents can provide reassurance.

- If a school wants to ensure good relations between the new intake and the rest of their cohort, they should involve other year groups in welcoming the new Year 7s. For example, at the taster day, it is good practice for prefects or older students to be responsible for the Year 6 students and help them out if they have any problems.

- If a school wants to maintain high standards, it will make these expectations clear from the outset. Students should come away from an induction day feeling they are valued, and that they will be challenged and supported to do their best.

- Some schools begin Year 7 with a programme of lessons similar to those found in primary schools. Others bring in the students' primary teachers to help in class. Others have early lessons in a single area giving students time to get used to the building's size.

- It is a good sign if a school has members of staff who have built up good relationships and contacts with local feeder* schools.

- If schools set* or stream* in subjects in Year 7, then they should use data from primary schools, combined with information gleaned themselves during the first half term or term. This means they are much more likely to group students correctly and start them off with work of appropriate challenge.

- A school that wants to combat the Year 7 'dip' will make sure that teachers have the Key Stage 2 SATs* results of their Year 7 students as soon as they are available. Teachers should then be planning their lessons around this data.

Further Information
Extra–curricular
Go to a school event organised by the PTA*. To find out when this might be, ring the school. When you are there, ask PTA members how they felt about transition arrangements for their child.
Open Evening/Visit
Ask to speak to someone who is responsible for transition or Year 7. Ask them to give you details about their induction and transition processes. Try and speak to a Year 7 pupil about what their transfer experience was like.
School Profile
A school might refer to good links with feeder schools in the section 'What have been our successes this year?'
School Publications
Ask the school to send you copies of correspondence sent to parents of prospective Year 7 students last year.

Case Study
Peter was very excited about learning when he was at primary school. He could be distracted in class, but for the most part he received very good reports, and achieved level* 5s in his Key Stage 2

SATs. He got a place at the secondary school where most of his friends went. It had a good reputation, but had become complacent, and was not on an upward trend.

On the taster day the staff did not seem to show much interest in the students. Peter actually found his taster lessons rather boring. All the exciting things he was looking forward to, like having a Science lesson in the laboratory, using the gym, and Drama studio were not part of the day. There was an assembly for all the new students, and Peter told his mother that it took the Head of Year* a long time to get everybody quiet. Peter did not meet the Head teacher on his taster day.

At lunchtime, Peter met a few older boys who were smoking at the back of the school. They were not unfriendly. In fact Peter was more excited by this event than anything else he had experienced that day. After this taster day, Peter began his secondary school career more excited about hanging around with the bigger boys, than his learning.

To sum up:
The right school for your child should try and make the transition from primary to secondary school mitigate against a dip in performance and the induction an experience which excites your child about learning.

'Beyond the School'

Alumni

It is worth investigating whether the schools you are considering have an alumni* organisation. It is undoubtedly a good sign if a school's ex students want to stay in touch with it and with each other.

- If a school has an alumni, or any kind of past students' organisation, this shows that ex students have a loyalty to the institution.
- If the school organises alumni events themselves, this shows that the institution is proud of its students' achievements
- An alumni organisation can inspire current students to be more ambitious, if they see successful role models who have passed through the same institution.
- A school with an alumni organisation usually has a sense of its own history and traditions. This is an important consideration if this is the kind of environment you want your child to be educated in.
- An alumni organisation often generates revenue. A better funded school usually means a better equipped school, able to offer a wider range of student provision.
- It is not a cause for concern if a school does not have an alumni organisation. However, if a school has no contact whatsoever with its ex students, it does suggest a lack of concern for students' futures and a lack of interest on the part of ex students in their old school.

- Even if a school does not have a formal alumni organisation, there are lots of ways it could be keeping in contact with some of its ex students. For example, they could come in to take assemblies, help out in lessons or, send their own children to the school. All of these things are a good sign.
- A school with a strong alumni tradition could give your child a sense of community long after their time at school has ended.

Further Information
Open Evening
Ask if the school an alumni organisation. Ask what events the school has which involve ex students. If the school does have an alumni group, ask if you can speak to one of its members – a recent ex student. If you do manage this, ask them why they want to stay in contact with the school – what do they see as the good things about the school? – what about the bad things? However, if you speak to a student who left a few years ago, remember how quickly schools can change.

To sum up:
Any positive contact a school has with its ex students is likely to benefit its current students.

Catchment Area

Not all schools have catchment* areas, and not all LEAs* have a catchment area system. It depends on their admissions procedure.

If a catchment area system is in place, this is potentially very expensive for parents, who will often move house to be in the catchment area of a popular school. It is rare that the catchment area for a popular school is composed of a cheap housing. The rules of supply and demand dictate that the more popular the school, the more expensive housing is in the catchment area.

Often, the more oversubscribed* the school is, the smaller the catchment area. If a school is less popular, it needs to spread its net further a field to fill its places.

- Schools that serve a local estate might not be right for your child, if you do not live on that estate.
- If you do live on an estate served by a local school, you might want to look further a field in order to find a greater breadth of social experiences for your child.
- Schools with a small catchment area often do not take in a diversity of children or parents.
- Schools which are oversubscribed, and as a consequence have a limited catchment area, might not necessarily be better than schools with a broader catchment area. Oversubscription is sometimes reliant on anecdotal information and inaccurate reputations.
- School is the place where your child is most likely to develop their social life. If you want your child's school social life to be accessible to them out of school hours, it is worth ensuring that you live in an area close to other students who attend the school. Also be sure

that the journey to school does not prohibit your child from taking part in after school extra-curricular* activities.

- It is important to investigate catchment areas. Do not take an estate agent's word for it. Your LEA pupil admissions* section should give you information about catchment arrangements and admission processes. They vary between local authorities. Many schools might not necessarily be taking from their closest environs, especially if the LEA prioritises students with siblings at the school over students who live in close proximity.

Further Information

Informal

If there are catchment areas, once you have found out where they are, drive round those which belong to schools you are interested in. This will help you get a feel of the social mix of the school's intake.

LEA

All LEAs will have an admissions pack which details their admissions policy, and any information on catchment areas, and over and undersubscription. The LEA will tell you which schools have their own admissions procedures, these might be, for example, academies* and faith* schools.

Case Study

School R had a good reputation and estate agents advertised houses as being in its catchment area. One family moved into the catchment area, as advised by an estate agent, incurring a hardly sustainable increase in their mortgage. It transpired that the LEA's admissions criteria prioritised sibling links over geographical proximity to the school. In fact there was no geographical catchment system in operation, proximity from school was measured according to transport arrangements. However, the parents did get their child into their chosen school. This was because the school's reputation was out of date and it moved from being an over to undersubscribed quickly. After a year at the school, the parents were dissatisfied with its provision and moved their child to a school they had previously not considered.

To sum up:
It is important to research catchment areas, before you make any decisions relating to them.

Local Media

The local media can sometimes be a good place to help research which school might be right for your child.

- It is a good sign if a school has a positive profile in the local media. If a school is regularly featured in a variety of upbeat stories, it shows that the school is pro-active, celebrates success and wants to get involved in the local community.
- If you read a story that puts the school in a negative light, it is important to read between the lines. If a crime takes place outside a school, it is not necessarily *a cause for concern*.

It is also common for students to go to another school to cause problems. If the article is about bullying, then it could be prompted by a parent who is bitter about treatment received from the school and is consequently distorting the facts.

- However, if over a 6 month period, there is a series of negative stories about a school in the local media, then this is *a cause for concern*.
- If the school does not feature in the local media at all, then that is not necessarily a bad thing. It does suggest that the school is not working hard to promote itself, but this might be because it feels it does not have to.

Further Information
Local Media
Look in the local paper for at least 6 months before you decide which school to send your child to, and monitor schools' representation in the press.

To sum up:
A school's local media profile can give you some idea about its achievements and desire for a high community profile.

Over/Under Subscription

Often an oversubscribed* school is a successful school. However, this may not be the whole story. An undersubscribed* school is not necessarily an unsuccessful school; and an oversubscribed school could be living on an out of date reputation.

LEA* admissions* packs will often tell you whether a school is over or undersubscribed. Sometimes this is one of the few pieces of information they give you about the school. This is because if a school is oversubscribed, the LEA may explain how places are allocated according to their admission priorities.

Because this is one of the few pieces of information issued, over or undersubscription is frequently given undue significance by parents choosing schools. Over or undersubscription needs to be understood in context.

An oversubscribed school can sometimes be living on an out of date reputation. Oversubscription sometimes becomes the focus for parents so that very little consideration is given to the current state of the school.

- An undersubscribed school could be making great improvements, but parents often fail to notice this because they are put off by the undersubscription.
- Undersubscribed schools often have greater obstacles to overcome to bring about improvement. Not least, that most school funding is generated by pupil numbers. If they manage to surmount these difficulties, then they are arguably more effective schools than oversubscribed schools because they achieve against greater odds.
- Oversubscribed schools have the advantage of only having students and parents who have chosen to go to their institution. Undersubscribed schools will normally have to take

many students whose first choice of school was elsewhere.

- When oversubscribed schools have vacancies, they usually have a waiting list. Officially, the schools have to apply their oversubscription criteria to the waiting list. However, unofficially, oversubscribed schools often manage to fill the school first with the students they most want.

- Undersubscribed schools always have vacancies. They cannot choose which students they take.

- If a student comes into the area and is not at the beginning of their secondary education, then they will be accepted at schools that have vacancies. Therefore undersubscribed schools often have greater instability with new students joining at an advanced stage in their secondary education.

- An undersubscribed school can sometimes turn into an institution for the students that an oversubscribed school would choose not to have.

Further Information

LEA

The LEA admissions booklet will tell you which schools are over or undersubscribed.

Ofsted

The 'Description of School' section will tell you whether the school was over or undersubscribed at the time of inspection.

Visit

Visit both an undersubscribed school and an oversubscribed school. If the application of the students in the classroom seems the same, then the under-subscribed school might be doing a better job. If levels of disruption seem greater in the undersub-scribed school, then it is probably not the right place for your child.

Case Study
A student teacher decided to carry out some obser-vations in two schools, one, an oversubscribed school in an affluent area, the other, an undersub-scribed school in a less affluent part of town. She was expecting to find the first school the easier option to work in. The oversubscribed school had a slightly higher value added* score than its under-subscribed counterpart, and much higher GCSE* results. However, the student teacher was surprised to find that student behaviour was significantly worse in the oversubscribed school. The teachers there put up with a much higher incidence of low level disruption. The student teacher deduced that this was because everybody had to try a lot less hard to get the results than in the undersubscribed school. In the undersubscribed school, the student teacher found that the students were expected to be more polite, and to work harder. Staff had more ideas and were less complacent. The student teacher decided to do her teaching practice in the undersubscribed school.

To sum up:
Investigate under and oversubscription – do not take it at face value and assume that oversubscrip-tion automatically means a school is better.

Reputation

A school's reputation is often the key factor determining parental choice. It is my experience that parents will often choose a school with a good reputation, without researching how genuine the reputation is.

- Reputations are sometimes generated by unreliable anecdotal evidence. For example, if one child is bullied, it does not necessarily mean that the school has a problem with bullying. If one child underachieves in their exams, it does not mean that this is the case for all students. If a serious incident happens outside the school, it might be the case that it has no connection with the institution itself. Students from one school invariably turn up at another school's entrance when they want to cause trouble.
- A school's reputation is often disseminated by its neighbours. However, they are not a reliable source. All schools cause disruption for those living next door. I rarely hear a school's neighbours say 'this is a good school', whatever its credentials.
- Oversubscription often depends on a reputation which is is not necessarily proof of a 'good' school, it is simply proof of enduring perceptions which may be inaccurate. There might be an 'emperor's new clothes' situation, with people following each other, without really questioning the quality of the school they are subscribing to.

- Reputations are often out of date. Schools can decline very quickly and reputations rarely keep up. Sometimes parents are responding to perceptions which were current when they were themselves at school.
- A parent needs to find a school that is improving. This school might actually be one that is living on an out of date 'bad' reputation. Choosing a school like this would be rather like buying property in an area, where there is going to be an increase in value.
- If a school's standards are rising, everyone is more enthusiastic, has more energy, and more creativity. If a school is declining, staff and students may be complacent, or have lost enthusiasm. Only an environment of positivity will breed success for students.

Further Information

Local Media

Look out for significant changes in your local schools which could lead to an out of date reputation. A change of Head, for example, may precipitate a rise or a decline, as could a change of building, or title.

Open Evening

Don't pre-judge schools, and only go to the open evening of the school with the best reputation. Visit a selection of schools in your catchment* area, so that you can compare what is on offer. Visit one school in your catchment area that has a 'bad' reputation. Even if it turns out that its reputation proves to be accurate, at least then you can measure it against your preference, and be reassured that you have made the right choice.

Prospectus, Achievement and Assessment Tables, Ofsted

If a school has a good reputation, confirm this by doing the research outlined in Chapter 2 of this book

Case Study

X School had a good reputation, and was the most popular amongst the 5 schools in the area. X School had been around along time. Parents in the area had gone to the school and, twenty years ago, it was the most popular local school. There were a lot of teachers at the school who had sent their own children to it, although none currently did. X School was the smallest secondary school in the area, so caused less disruption to its neighbours than larger schools.

However, Achievement and Assessment Tables* showed that the 5 or more A*–C percentage had reduced year on year for the last 3 years. This decline was not obvious, because the school still got a higher percentage than any of its neighbours, although 3 of the neighbouring schools' percentages were on the increase.

The Head teacher had been at the school for fifteen years, and was well known in the local community, but was biding his time until his retirement.

Within 5 years, X School went into special measures*. Results plummeted, the A*–C percentage halved. Meanwhile, 3 of the other schools in the neighbourhood had overtaken X School's A*–C percentage. It was only 2 Head teachers and 5 years later that the school began to improve again.

To sum up:
Reputation alone is not enough to make a decision about what might be the right school for your child, because it is frequently subjective and inaccurate. If the school is on the up, you want to get in before the rush to join sets in, if it is on the decline, you want to avoid it.

School Publications

A school will have a variety of publications that you can access to find out about the school.

- All school publications should have a consistent finish. For example, they should all feature a school logo, and all letters should adhere to a standard format. If presentation is sloppy and inconsistent then this could suggest a lack of attention to detail or pride and is *a cause for concern*.
- A school's publications should not contain errors. It is *a cause for concern* if a communication contains spelling or grammatical mistakes.
- All communications should be accessible to the school's cohort. Therefore, if a number of languages are spoken at home by its students, key communications should be issued in translation.
- A school should have all its publications readily available for the public. If you phone and ask for the latest newsletter to be sent to you, this should be no trouble.
- A school should have a planned communica-

tion strategy. It should not be common practice for unplanned letters to be sent last minute. If replies are required, appropriate return times should be given. Publications should not send out conflicting information.

- A constantly updated and accessible school diary of events should be available.
- It is a good sign if a school has a publication which has substantial input from students, for example, a school magazine or year book. This demonstrates that the student voice is valued, that a variety of extra-curricular activities are available, and that students' communication skills are stretched.
- A year book can foster a sense of community and tradition. It cultivates an audience who feel part of the institution and it can strengthen a school's sense of identity. It can create a history for the school as volumes build up and ex students keep their year book as a memento of their time at the school.
- A school with a specialism should demonstrate this through their publications. So an Arts and Media school might produce a DVD for prospective students.

Newsletter

It is unusual for a school not to have a newsletter of some sort with which it communicates with its parents.

A good newsletter should:

- be read by parents. It is good sign if the newsletter has inclusions which demonstrate parent engagement, for example, a parent response section.

- be regular. Out of date news serves little purpose.
- reflect the diversity of its student and parent readership. All abilities of students should be represented as should multi-culturalism where appropriate.
- reflect the whole school and not focus on one subject area. A variety of subject areas, extra-curricular activities and staff should feature.
- be informative. Parents should be regularly informed of impending events and dates.
- be entertaining and go out of its way to engage its readers with photographs, and a variety of features.
- If the school is a specialist college, then this should be apparent in its newsletter. For example, a Techology College should have a communication with a high finish, an Arts College's newsletter should feature high quality Art inputs.

Website

A website does not define a good school. However, a school website can certainly be useful in giving you more information about whether the school is the right school for your child.

- Websites are increasingly the norm and you should expect to find one.
- A specialist Technology College should have a

website, if it is taking its status seriously.

- In many ways a website can be interpreted in a similar way to a prospectus. In fact many schools have their prospectus available in electronic form on the website.

- A website that is easy to access shows the school is concerned with communicating effectively with key groups, for example, parents, students, governors and the local community.

- It is important to determine what the website is for. Is it just for show, or is it for use. Sections which are clearly actively used by staff, parents and students are a good sign. Questions to parents like 'Need an up to date school calendar click here' show that the website is responding directly to parental needs.

- If the website is not up to date, then it is possible that the school does not have a good record of following through projects that it has started.

- It is a good sign if there are areas on the website that are live and working, for example, up to date bulletin boards and diaries.

- The level of student involvement in the site tells you a lot about the school. If the website was devised by the students themselves then that is a very good sign. Sections such as 'student voice' which, for example, have current minutes from school councils, show the school in action and are a good sign.

- It is a good sign if the site includes work from students. However, make sure the work is up to date.

Further Information
School Publications
Ask a school for the last four editions of its newsletter and copies of all the letters it has sent out to Year 7* in the last term.
Open Evening
If the school does have a website, then ask what input students have into it. Ask if the school has a year book or school magazine and request a copy.

To sum up:
School publications should consistently reflect high standards, good organisation and a strong institutional identity.

'The Issues'

Behaviour and Discipline

Behaviour and discipline should be key factors in determining your choice of school. Poor student behaviour means a lack of boundaries, security, and access to equality of opportunity for your child. If students are poorly behaved, it is likely that the teacher will expend more time on those who are disrupting, than on those behaving well.

It is tempting for a child to join in with poor behaviour rather than stay on task. When I have interviewed students, the most common reason they give for misbehaviour is the fact that their friends misbehave. A child's friendship groups usually have a greater influence on their actions than their desire to achieve. If behaviour is poor in the classroom there is no guarantee, whatever your expectations of your child, that they will behave well.

A school that has cracked behaviour and discipline is most likely to give your child a fair chance at reaching their potential.

- Good discipline is largely determined by the teacher. In the right school for your child, the majority of teachers must be good disciplinarians.
- Good disciplinarians are not necessarily teachers who shout or are aggressive. The best disciplinarian is a teacher who can maintain control through a calm, confident manner.
- Well behaved classes are not necessarily those

which work in silence. In fact, the best classes for learning are often where there is work related talk going on, but when silence is needed, it must be easily attained and maintained.

- Every school, no matter how successful, will have some teachers who are weak disciplinarians. However, the school should have an overall ethos of good discipline and behaviour, which counteracts the limitations of individual staff.
- Most schools have a behaviour code or policy. To be of any value, it must be put into action.
- Some schools have a behaviour code that is drawn up with the students and on display in every classroom. To involve students in defining a code is a positive step, but only if it is consistently carried out. Many schools have a clear and easily understood list of rules. If they are internalised by the students and applied by staff, then they are likely to be effective.
- There must be a behaviour and discipline structure that works and that the students believe in. Children must know that if they misbehave, clear sanctions will be enacted. They must understand that the sanctions become progressively more serious, and that they will, in due course, be referred to more senior staff. Students must not believe that they can get away with things.
- If there is a culture where low levels of misbehaviour are not dealt with properly, then this will undermine effective teaching and learning. There should be attention to detail. If the

details are taken care of, then the big picture will fall into place. For example, if a school insists that students take their coats off in class and an individual teacher fails to apply this rule, then this teacher has no purchase over the students if they commit a greater misdemeanour.

- Students should always follow the reasonable requests of teachers.
- Misbehaviour should be the exception to the rule, never the norm.
- Every school must have a 'bottom line' member of senior management*, with whom, as far as the students are concerned, if they misbehave, the buck stops. This might be the Head teacher, or a Deputy. This person should have such a reputation, that the students would rather anything else happened, than be sent to them.
- Student behaviour is usually good, if there is a visible senior staff presence which deters children from misbehaving. In some schools, as teachers get promoted to Assistant Head teacher, Deputy or Head, they deal less and less with students. This is not a good model. If good behaviour is to be maintained consistently then the senior team must have a hands on approach to behaviour and discipline.
- In the right school for your child, the senior team should be seen everywhere. There should be no corner of the school, nor time of the school day where and when students think they can misbehave. The senior team should be visible at lesson changeover times, at the beginning and the end of break times and at

the school gate at the beginning and end of the day. They should be talking to and challenging students all the time.

- The Head teacher must have the strength and the confidence to levy strong sanctions for serious misdemeanours. If a Head teacher balks at giving out serious sanctions, students will believe that they can get away with things.

- Sanctions should be consistent and clear. Students should know, for example, that if they swear at a teacher, then clear action will be taken. If such an incident occurs, then the whole class should immediately be confident that serious action will follow which identifies the culprit, and punishes them appropriately. It is no good if there is a climate where if a teacher is sworn at, the students think something might happen, but on a given day, it might not.

- It is *a cause for concern* if all staff do not see it as their individual and collective responsibility to maintain good behaviour. In this climate, students will think they can misbehave if certain staff are present. They will not get a consistent message. In the right school for your child all staff will take on the mantle of maintaining discipline and behaviour at all times.

- Sanctions should in part be dependent on a student's record. For example, the first time a student swears at a teacher, a fixed exclusion of a certain number of days could be meted out to them. If the student offends again, then the temporary exclusion should be lengthened. When the student swears for a second time at the teacher, the rest of the class should be clear that they are in greater trouble, because this misdemeanour has happened before.

- It is *a cause for concern* if staff are afraid of students. Sometimes in schools there is a small core of students that most staff do not challenge because they are concerned about confrontation or retaliation. Staff think that if they challenge these students, they will be abused. The right school for your child needs to be somewhere where all staff feel empowered to take on all students. There will never be a school that is free of rudeness or back chat. But there are schools where if a student does talk back to a teacher who challenges them, the teacher knows that the behaviour system will support them, and further action will be taken. If a teacher feels supported, they will consistently challenge students appropriately.

Further Information
Open Evening/Visits
Look for school rules or a code of conduct in every classroom. Then look to see these implemented at first hand during your visit.

Ask a pupil, what would happen to them if they, for example, spoke back to a teacher. You want an answer that makes it quite clear that students get into trouble for this, and that it does not happen regularly. It is *a cause for concern* if you find out that 'nothing really happens'.

Ask students if there are certain rules – things that they know they cannot do, for example, chew gum in class. If they say 'yes', and in most classes and school areas, this rule is adhered to, then that is a good sign. Remember that there will always be some glitches in any well applied system. If however, students are aware of no such rules, then this is *a cause for concern*. It is also not a good sign if they acknowledge such rules exist but admit they are rarely or inconsistently applied.

Make sure you see the school in action. In the majority of the lessons, children should be on task, and there should not be students roaming unsupervised around the corridors. It is *a cause for concern* if you see students misbehaving and a teacher either being ignored or ignoring the misdemeanour. It is not a problem if, on occasion, you see misbehaviour. In fact, it shows you are seeing the school as it really is. What is a problem is if the bad behaviour is not always addressed.

Case Study

In School T the Head teacher avoided disciplining the students. He saw his job as being largely administrative, and felt that discipline should be left solely to Heads of Year*. He did not have anybody else in his senior team, whose authority students respected. His office door was closed most of the time, and many students did not know who he was.

Treatment of misbehaviour was inconsistent. In Maths, students received a detention from the Head of Department*, whom they respected, so they generally behaved. In Art, however, they would receive a quiet word from the Deputy Head of Department whom they did not respect. In the majority of classes, students who misbehaved got more attention; a minority intimidated the teacher and the other students. Therefore standards were inconsistent. There was no clear referral system which the students and staff trusted; and there was no 'bottom line' member of the senior team, with whom the buck stopped.

The school got a new Head teacher, whose forte was pupil discipline. On the first day of her appointment, she got out and about, and showed the students who was boss. She set up a very clear system of referral, so all misdemeanours carried a clear punishment, and she was the ultimate discipline enforcer. Children saw that if their peers crossed a boundary, something happened. Although the Head teacher rarely raised her voice, the students respected her and dreaded being referred to her. Behaviour improved dramatically in the school. The vast majority of students were on task and prioritising learning.

To sum up:
The right school for your child should do its best to deliver a sense of security and equality of opportunity in the classroom. A strong behaviour and discipline system contributes to this.

Bullying

One of the greatest concerns for parents is likely to be bullying. It is an unfortunate fact, that no school is totally free from bullying. However, there are key things to look out for which show that a school is effectively tackling the problem.

- If you are told by a school that no bullying goes on in their institution, they are quite simply not telling you the truth.
- Your best gauge as to how much bullying goes on is to ask the students themselves on a school visit.
- A solid pastoral* system often mitigates against bullying. Bullying is more likely to occur in a school where the students do not have faith in the ability of teachers to sort things out for them. A good pastoral system means that students will tell teachers if they are being bullied, without fear of the teacher making things worse.
- Find out whether your child will have a tutor* who is approachable and interested in their welfare. A good tutor develops a sense of belonging and responsibility in her form group, so that students look out for each other. You also want a school where the year or house system actually works – where there is a Head of Year or House* who can take effective action against bullying and whom the students trust.
- A school should always have an anti-bullying policy with which teachers and students must be familiar. If there is no policy at all, then that is *a cause for concern*. However, I have been in schools where the policy is papered every-where, but it is not a living document that anyone takes notice of. It is effective action that counts, not words.
- There are various initiatives run by schools which can reduce the chances of bullying occurring. Older students who have been

trained as counsellors or mentors often provide effective support. A buddy system between older and younger students is sometimes adopted by schools, and prefect systems can be very effective, if the prefects protect younger students from bullying rather than instigating it themselves. Indeed, any process which encourages older students to look after the younger children is advantageous. Some schools have a vertical tutor group system, where groups contain students from all year groups. This system is often effective in reducing bullying.

- A school that is serious about creating a safe environment for its students should have a student council where student representatives are consulted by staff on key issues. In many schools the student council is weak. Students don't take it seriously, and the discussions never get beyond paper in the girls' toilets. However, a successful student council can really make students feel that they have a voice that is counted, and they can trust the process to address issues as serious as bullying.

- Schools that take the time to listen to students are more likely to combat bullying effectively. For example, if schools have an annual self evaluation process, which involves questioning students, they are likely to pick up bullying issues, such as when and where bullying happens, which might otherwise go unnoticed.

- Schools are required to deliver the subject of Citizenship*. Usually, it is taught as a discrete subject, or it maybe integrated into other subject areas. Bullying is something that should be covered by the Citizenship curriculum in some form. In some schools, Citizenship is not taken sufficiently seriously. In this context, the inclusion of bullying as a curriculum issue will have little effect on the wider school. To ensure Citizenship is taken more seriously schools sometimes employ a specialist Citizenship teacher, make the subject a GCSE* option, or stage whole school extra-curricular* events related to Citizenship, for example, anti-bullying drama productions. In this atmosphere, the inclusion of an anti bullying message as an aspect of the curriculum may have more impact.

- Bullying often takes place if the school has 'no go' areas, where students are in control and teachers rarely patrol. A school serious about the threat of bullying should be constantly working to make all areas safe, open and accessible. Teachers should be visible, and the environment should be well maintained.

Further Information
Open Evening
Ask to speak to a teacher who is also a tutor. Ask them about what strategies they use to combat bullying. You want to get a sense of whether tutors take on board the issue of bullying at a grass roots level, or leave it to someone else to sort out. You also want to get an idea of whether this is a school where tutors take an active interest in their tutor group, or whether the pastoral curriculum is just tokenistic.

Find the teacher responsible for Citizenship and ask about how it is taught – is the topic of bullying included in the curriculum?

Look out for a code of conduct or set of school rules on display. This should include an anti-bullying statement. It should be prominent in all classrooms. If it is not, ask why.

Questions to ask the Head teacher:

Do you have an anti-bullying policy, and how do you implement it?

How do you actively tackle bullying at this school?

Questions to ask the Head of Year or House:

What do you do if one of your year group comes to you and says that they are bullied?

Does the school have a student council, and what does it do?

School Profile

The section 'What have pupils told us about the school' may include information about a student council.

Visit

Ask the student who is showing you round about bullying. Ask if they have ever suffered from it. Ask how the older students get on with the younger students. Ask the student what they would do if they got bullied and what the school does if someone gets bullied. You want to find out whether students have faith in the system and actually report bullying, because they have an expectation that the school can sort it out for them.

Ask the student whether there are any 'no go' areas, which they avoid because of the threat of bullying.

When you are walking around the school, ask your student guide to take you to the backs of buildings, where staff are least likely to go. It is obviously *a cause for concern* if you experience an atmosphere of threat when you visit these areas. Look out for graffiti and cigarette butts – signs that areas are not regularly supervised.

Case Study
B School had a high profile bullying policy which had been created in collaboration with a well known charity. Two students had been on television talking about how there was no bullying at their school. The bullying policy was in every room, printed on high quality coloured paper and laminated. When asked at open evening, the Head teacher said he had zero tolerance for bullying.

At the side of the school was an area where there was no student seating or creative planting. There was no security camera. That is where the Year 10 boys took the Year 8 boys to extort money. The boys saw it as part of the school system and nobody complained. The Head teacher had not walked around that part of the school in the last six months.

To sum up:
Unfortunately, bullying takes place in every school. What you as a parent need to find out is whether it is effectively dealt with, and whether there is a school ethos which counters it.

Security and Safety

In recent years there have been tragic incidences of fatal attacks upon students, some on school sites. These have led in part to calls for improved school security such as 'airport style' scanners to seek out knives. However, most of the high profile cases you will recall have actually taken place outside schools, albeit involving students. This is not to diminish the risk to young people in schools and the right school for your child must clearly have security as a priority. However, parents should not overreact to fears about school safety.

It is also worth pointing out that no school, no matter how successful they are, is completely free from threat. A balance must be struck between security and the need for schools to be buildings which welcome their local community.

What is important is how schools identify security risks and implement consistent and common sense approaches to counter them.

- If a school is regularly permanently excluding students for carrying knives or other weapons, then this is *a cause for concern*; it indicates that there is a culture of carrying weapons at the school.
- A school should have a clear policy on sanctions to be taken if a child is found carrying a weapon – if this policy seems inadequate or vague, then this is *a cause for concern*.
- It is *a cause for concern* if there is a gang culture at a school, even though gang related incidents usually take place out of the school

arena. Schools where there are gangs are likely to have an intake from clearly defined geographical areas. If a school takes the majority of its students from two or three specific areas, for example, estates, then gangs that are formed on the streets can come into the school. If a school has only a few large primary feeder* schools, then it might be that alliances established at primary school are perpetuated in secondary and exacerbated as children grow older.

- Most schools have ample security to help protect students from strangers entering their site. There should be a system to help ensure strangers do not access the site, for example, a school gate that requires a code for entry. At the reception, a signing in process should be in place. There should be systems for monitoring the whole school building, for example, security cameras.

- You may find that some schools employ guards. This is potentially *a cause for concern*. You will need to ask why this unusual level is security is necessary.

- A secure school should maintain its boundaries well. Holes in fences should be constantly repaired; trees and shrubs should be regularly cut back.

- There should be a system of entering and exiting which is clear to the students and which they abide by. For example, if there is an entrance for staff only, students should not be seen sneaking in that way.

- A secure school should work collaboratively

with its neighbours. If, for example, it shares facilities with a neighbouring leisure centre, the entrances to the two venues should be clearly separate.

- A secure school has a good caretaker. She is diligent, knows her school and where the weakest links are, and maintains security systems.
- A secure school is careful about who uses the building apart from its students. All other site use is by formal arrangement. Its security is not so lax that youths from other schools play football on its grounds, out of hours without permission.
- A secure school has visible staff at the school gates, whenever students are officially entering and exiting.
- Some schools have a school based police officer. This can be a successful system if the officer is capable and has the capacity to support the school.
- All schools should be up to date with Criminal Record Bureau checks for their staff, both teaching and non-teaching.

Further Information
Open Evenings/Visit
Ask to speak to the caretaker. Ask her how she deals with security issues at the school.

Ask a senior teacher what the school's main primary feeders are.

Make sure you visit the school in the day time. At reception you should be asked to sign in and out, and given some form of visitor identification.

Make an informal visit. Go and walk round the school out of hours; are there 'rogue' youths in the playgrounds, or are there organised groups using the facilities?

Find out when school starts and finishes. Walk round the school and see if staff are visible. See if the boundaries of the site are maintained, or are there students, for example, climbing through holes in fences.

Ask if the school is up to date with its Criminal Record Bureau checks for staff.

LEA

The LEA* admissions* booklet should give you information about catchment* areas and this will help you to determine which are the primary feeder schools.

To sum up:

No school is a completely safe environment, whatever steps are taken. You must be reassured that systems are in place that appear appropriate to security risks and that the degree of risk in your school of preference is not unusually high.

Chapter 4

The Application

- Every council has a local education authority LEA*.
- In every LEA there is an admissions* department which is responsible for pupil admissions to that authority.
- You will locate your admissions department on your LEA's website, or by phoning your local council.

The LEA issues an admissions booklet and an application form. Usually these are distributed through primary schools but you can request copies directly from the LEA.

- In most authorities the application and admissions process begins in September the year before your child starts secondary school.
- Most authorities will request that the application form be completed by about the end of October the year before your child starts secondary school.
- In all authorities you will be asked to list at least

three secondary school preferences.
- In all authorities you will receive your offer of a place no later than 1st March of the year that your child starts secondary school. You will receive the offer of only one school.

The LEA will usually handle applications to all their schools through a central application form. Some schools will require you to complete a supplementary form along with the central form. Normally, you can get the supplementary form directly from those schools. The schools that require a supplementary form are usually those that select and academies*.

The vast majority of state schools do not select. However, some schools have selection or preference criteria:

- Grammar schools select by ability.
- Church or faith* schools are allowed to select according to a particular faith or denomination. Some academies are church schools.
- Specialist* schools are allowed to select 10% of their students according to ability in the specialism, although the majority of them do not.

What's In the Admissions Booklet:

- Whether a school is under or oversubscribed* will have a big impact on its admissions. LEA booklets often tell you whether each school is over or undersubscribed. The admissions booklet will tell you how many applications each school had the year before and how many applicants were successful.

- If a school does not select, is undersubscribed and is your first preference, then you should be allocated this school.
- If a school is oversubscribed then each LEA has its own priority list of admission criteria. These are largely dictated by national guidelines, but do vary between LEAs. The priority categories for admission, beginning with the highest, are likely to be:

1. Children in care.
2. Children with a statement of special needs*.
3. Children who live nearest to the school/in the catchment* area.
4. Children with siblings at the school.
5. All other children.

- Schools that select are likely to have their own priority list that links with their priority or selection criteria.
- Most authorities operate catchment area systems for schools. If they do operate a catchment system however, this does not guarantee you a place if you live in that catchment. It depends on the nature and number of applications for a school each year.
- Some authorities do not operate catchment areas, but use the 'nearest to the school' system. With this system, the more oversubscribed the school is, the shorter the distance of residence from the school for acceptance.

- Some authorities maintain waiting lists for schools. These are maintained in the order of their oversubscription criteria. This information should be explained in the LEA admissions booklet.
- Some LEAs use a banding* system. They allocate students to bands according to their ability and then schools are allocated a certain number of students from each band to help ensure a comprehensive intake.
- If you want to apply for a school outside the LEA where you live, every LEA will operate its own system for managing such requests.
- LEAs cannot and do not offer a first come first served admissions process. There is no advantage in getting your application in early.
- Church schools are allowed to interview prospective students and their parents to assess religious commitment. Otherwise, state schools are not allowed to use interviews to assess applicants.
- It is important to note that the Head teacher does not 'choose' their students. In some situations, such as that of church schools, the governing body makes decisions on admissions issues. The Head teacher is likely to be a member of the governing body, but cannot make decisions on their own.

Further Information

www.cesew.org.uk
The Catholic Education Service website contains information about Catholic schools and has a school-finder facility.

www.cofe.anglican.org
This is the Church of England website which gives you information about Church of England schools.

www.directgov.uk
Produced by the Central Office of Information, Directgov provides information from across UK government departments on topics ranging from travel safety and parental leave to special educational needs and local NHS services. It has a short, informative section on 'Choosing a School'.

www.ngsa.org.uk
This is the site of the National Grammar School Association, a non-political body promoting grammar schools in England.

www.ofsted.gov.uk
This is where you can find Ofsted reports of any

school you might be considering, up to twenty miles from the postcode input.

www.parentscentre.gov.uk
This is site run for parents by the DfES. It has a useful section on 'Choosing Schools' which is broken down into the following sections:

- admissions and applications
- types of school
- school performance
- local authorities
- finding the right school

It also has a link to help you find schools in your area, and access the relevant Achievement and Assessment Tables, Ofsted reports, and School Profiles.

www.raisingkids.co.uk
This is a site aimed at giving parents support and advice on bringing up children. It has a short section on how to choose a school for your child.

www.standards.dfes.gov.uk
This is a DFES website, primarily aimed at school professionals, but useful for clear and concise information on all aspects of schools, for example, gifted and talented students or academies.

www.yourlocalauthority.gov.uk
Each local authority has a website whose address will be as above. This website will have a separate section on secondary education, and will always have a link to pupil admissions.

www.goodschoolsguide.co.uk
This is a website which is linked to the publication 'The Good Schools' Guide' which reviews individual state and private schools, and can be purchased from the site, or accessed electronically for a fee. However, the site also offers a free search for schools in your area.

Glossary

Words or acronyms that are asterisked* in the book are listed in this glossary.

'A' Levels
'A' Levels are one of the qualifications that students can do in the 6th form, Years 12 and 13*. They are split into two parts, AS and A2. 'A' Levels are considered to be an academic qualification. Most degree courses at universities stipulate that students should have three 'A' Levels at particular grades.

Academic Review
Academic Review is a form of parental consultation, often in lieu of parents' evening*. Parents come to an event where they meet their child's tutor* and set targets to help their child to improve.

Academies
Academies are privately sponsored, but are still state schools. Previously failing schools which have closed are often re-launched as Academies. They are often new build.

Achievement and Assessment Tables

Also known as 'League Tables' and 'School Performance Tables'.

These are the national tables which classify schools in order of their examination results. Schools are grouped according to what local authority they are in. There are two league tables published each year.

One table focuses on the percentage of students at each school who score five or more, or the equivalent, GCSEs grades A*–C. From 2006, along side the A*–C statistic will be the percentage of students achieving five or more grades A*–C, including English and Maths GCSE and from 2007 this will replace the previous statistic.

The other table publishes the Key Stage 3* SATs* results at each school.

Admissions

Admissions is the department in the local education authority responsible for allocating children to schools.

Aim Higher

Aim Higher is an initiative funded by the government in certain schools. It supports students from under privileged backgrounds who have the potential to go to university.

Alumni

Alumni are the school's ex students. An alumni organisation might stage events, for example, reunions, or publish a newsletter for ex-students.

Assistant Head Teacher
An Assistant Head teacher is a senior manager. They are usually below Deputy Head teachers* in school hierarchies.

Average Point Score
When students apply for a place in higher education, each pass grade they obtain in certain qualifications scores a certain number of points.

Banding
Also known as 'streaming'.

Banding is a way of organising students into ability groups. Banding means that students are put into the same ability groups for most or all subjects. So if a student is in the top band for Maths, they will also be in the top band for other subjects, like English and Science.

Banding is also a method some local authorities use to ensure that students from different ability groups are represented in all their comprehensive schools.

BSF – Building Schools for the Future
All secondary schools are involved in the government programme BSF. Its aim is to rebuild or renew every secondary school in England over the next 10-15 year period.

BTEC
BTEC is a vocational qualification which is replacing GNVQs* from 2006. It is graded mainly by ongoing assessment. BTECs are undertaken at Key Stages 4 and 5*. They are equivalent to 2 or 4 GCSEs*

depending on the level of depth in which a student studies the course.

Careers
The subject of Careers consists of information and guidance provided to students on employment options.

Catchment
A school's catchment is the locality from where a school is most likely to take their students.

CATs – Cognitive Ability Tests
CATs are given to students to help schools to predict their academic potential. For example, a CATs test could predict that a student is capable of attaining five or more A*–C grades at GCSE*. CATs tests are usually given to students in Years 7 and 9*. They are often used to work out whether schools have added value* or not.

CDT – Craft & Design Technology
See 'DT'

Child Protection
Child protection issues concern children at risk in their home environment, for example, from abuse or neglect.

Citizenship
Citizenship is taught to all year groups. Its role is to inform students about how to be active citizens. All students have to do Citizenship as a non-examination subject, but some schools run a GCSE* or other

external accreditation in Citizenship.

Classroom Assistants
Also known as 'Teaching Assistants (TAs)', 'Higher Level Teacher Assistants (HLTAs)', 'Special Needs Assistants (SNAs)', 'Support staff'.

Assistants support teachers in and out of the lesson working with particular students, for example, those with special educational needs*. At the time of writing, there are moves towards Classroom Assistants taking parts of a lesson without a teacher present.

Comprehensive Schools
Comprehensives are state schools which admit a cross section of students from the community with a range of academic abilities.

Core Subjects
Core subjects at secondary school are those which must be studied by all students, for example, English, Maths and Science.

Day Book
See 'journal'.

Deputy Head Teacher
A Deputy Head teacher is a senior manager. They are usually above Assistant Head teachers* in school hierarchies and, as their title suggests, deputise for the Head teacher in their absence.

DfES – Department for Education and Skills
The DfES is the government department with

responsibility for education.

Directed Time
Directed time is the number of hours that teachers are legally required to work at the Head teacher's direction each year, currently 1265 hours. It does not include time spent on planning, preparation and marking.

DT – Design & Technology
DT is the name given by some schools to the study of practical based technology skills. It is a National Curriculum* subject, and should contain Resistant Materials* Food Technology* and Textiles* although these areas will normally be taught separately.

Dyslexia
Dyslexia is a learning disability affecting reading capacity.

Dyspraxia
Dyspraxia is a learning difficulty in performing tasks requiring fine motor skills such as drawing or writing.

EAL – English as an Additional Language
See 'EMAG'

EBD – Emotional and Behavioural Difficulties
This classification includes a range of needs. For example, an EBD student might find it difficult to behave appropriately in a school environment.

EMAG – Ethnic Minority Achievement Grant
EMAG students are from ethnic minorities and receive additional support to assist them in accessing the National Curriculum.

Equal Opportunities Policy
This is a policy which states how the school will try and treat all students fairly and give them equal access to the school curriculum and other activities.

Excellence in Cities
Excellence in Cities is a government initiative to provide additional support to schools in certain deprived urban areas.

Exclusions
The most serious sanctions a school can use are fixed term or permanent exclusions. 'Fixed term' exclusions are sometimes called suspensions. Usually, after a large number of fixed term exclusions, a student will be permanently excluded. Or a school may impose a permanent exclusion for one very serious misdemeanour. A school may use fixed term exclusions quite regularly, but permanent exclusions are usually only given in extreme circumstances.

Extended Schools
Extended Schools provide a range of services in addition to traditional school provision. For example, child care or evening classes for adults. By 2010 all schools will be extended schools.

Extra-curricular
Extra-curricular activities take place outside of lesson times, for example, at lunchtime or after school.

FE – Further Education
FE is education at 6th form level, Years 12 and 13*.

First Schools
First Schools are part of the middle school* system and they take students from Years 1 to 4.

Foundation Schools
Foundation schools have opted out of local authority control. They have more control over their budget, governance and admissions* than other state schools.

Foundation Subjects
Foundation subjects are not tested through SATs* but schools are required to teach, assess and report upon them at the end of Key Stage 3*. They include History, Geography, Music and Design Technology.

Free School Meals
Free School meals' percentages are used to help gauge the number of students from deprived backgrounds who go to a school. Parents have to be in receipt of benefits for their children to qualify for free school meals.

FT – Food Technology
FT is the study of cookery, food hygiene and menu planning. It is part of the Design Technology* subject group.

GCSE – General Certificate of Secondary Education

GCSEs are the key qualification students take at Key Stage 4*, when they are 16. They replaced 'O' Levels. Most schools make English, Maths and Science GCSEs obligatory. GCSEs have grades from A*–U. In the eyes of schools, colleges and the government, a 'C' grade is in effect a pass, a 'D' grade or below is a fail. Many further education* courses demand that students achieve five GCSEs at grades A*–C.

Gifted and Talented

Gifted and Talented students are those considered to be the most academically able in the school. Some schools have a gifted and talented programme funded directly by the government, others a programme that they fund themselves.

GNVQ – General National Vocational Qualification

GNVQ is a vocational* qualification which students normally take at the end of Key Stage 4* when they are 16. A GNVQ is worth 2 or 4 GCSEs*. GNVQs will be phased out by 2007 and replaced by the BTEC* qualification.

Governors

Every school has a governing body. They are a group of volunteers chosen by parents, the local authority, the community and school staff. They are responsible for strategic and legal aspects of the school's work. The governing body line manages the Head teacher. Governors should oversee the annual summary of the school's progress and achievements for parents called the School Profile*.

Graduate Teacher
A graduate teacher carries out school based teacher training.

Grammar Schools
State grammar schools are selective schools. They have an entrance test, often still called the 11 plus exam, which selects the most academic students. Relatively few areas still have grammar schools.

Graphics
Graphics is the study of aspects of design using drawing and computer technology. It is part of the Design and Technology* subject group but is often found as a separate subject at Key Stage 4*. It was traditionally known as technical drawing.

HE – Higher Education
HE is education at degree level or equivalent, normally undertaken after the 6th form.

Head of Department
Each subject area usually has a Head of Department, for example, a Head of History. Larger subject areas often have Deputy Heads of Department. Some schools have Heads of Faculty, meaning the Head of a group of subjects. A Head of Department or Faculty is responsible for the teaching and learning in their particular subject area(s).

Head of Faculty
See 'Head of Department'.

Head of Year/Head of House

A student will be in a year group from Years 7 to 11 or 13*. They might also be in a House*. A House is a team that students are organised into, usually for reasons of group loyalty or inter group competition. The Head of Year or House is responsible for a year group or House.

The Head of Year usually progresses up the school with their year group, eventually becoming their Head of Year 11. Less commonly, Heads of Year remain stationary while the students move on, for example, a static Head of Year 7. Heads of 6th form are normally specialist posts.

The Head of Year or House is usually responsible for results, behaviour and the moral and social welfare of students. After the tutor*, the Head of Year or House is the first person a parent would contact about their child.

Healthy Schools

Healthy Schools status is a government programme through which schools can be accredited if they address certain priorities related to students' physical and emotional well being.

HLTAs – Higher Level Teaching Assistants

See 'Classroom Assistants'.

House

A House is a team that groups of students are organised into for reasons of motivation and camaraderie. Houses usually stretch across year groups.

See also 'Head of Year/Head of House.'

ICT – Information and Communication Technology

ICT is the aspect of the curriculum where students work with and learn about computers and related technology. It was previously known as IT.

Independent Schools

Also known as 'Private Schools', 'Public Schools'*.

Independent schools are fee paying, privately run schools.

Journal

Also known as 'day book', or 'diary'.

Most schools give students a school journal. It is used primarily for recording homework, and facilitating communication between home and school. The journal usually has a place where parents and tutors* can sign every week, to say they have read the homework set and acknowledged any communications with each other.

KS2 – Key Stage 2

Key Stage 2 is the learning stage from Year 4* age 8/9 to Year 6* age 10/11, at primary school. At the end of Key Stage 2, students take national SATs* exams in English, Maths and Science.

KS3 – Key Stage 3

Key Stage 3 is the learning stage from Year 7* age 11/12 to Year 9* age 14, at secondary school. At the end of Key Stage 3, students take national SATs* exams in English, Maths and Science. They are also given a Key Stage 3 level by their teacher in the foundation* subjects.

KS4 – Key Stage 4
Key Stage 4 is the learning stage from Year 10* age 15 to Year 11* age 16. At the end of Key Stage 4 students take GCSEs*, GNVQs* or BTECs*.

KS5 – Key Stage 5
Key Stage 5 encompasses Years 12 and Year 13*, or the 6th form*. Here students take 'A' Levels* or equivalent vocational qualifications, such as BTEC*.

LEA – Local Education Authority
The LEA is in charge of delivering education for the council in a borough or county.

League Tables
See 'Achievement and Assessment Tables'.

Learning Mentors
Also known as 'Mentors'

Learning Mentors are employed by schools to support students encountering social or organisational difficulties which are hindering their studies.

Levels
At Key Stage 2* and Key Stage 3* students are awarded National Curriculum levels to measure academic progress. The levels go from level 1 to level 8. In Year 9*, level 5 is the average nationally.

Mentors
See 'Learning Mentors'.

MFL – Modern Foreign Languages
MFL is the study of foreign languages at secondary school.

Midday Assistants
Midday assistants are non teaching staff employed to supervise students during their breaks and lunchtimes.

Middle Schools
Middle schools take students from Years 5 to 8*, age 9 to 13. Some boroughs or counties have a system where all students go from a primary or first* school, to a middle school to a high school at the age of 13. A few boroughs or counties have a junior and secondary school system in the main, with a few middle schools.

Mixed Ability
Mixed Ability is a system of organising students into teaching groups, with a range of academic abilities in one classroom.

National Curriculum
The National Curriculum consists is those subjects and programmes of study that schools are legally required to provide.

Ofsted – Office for Standards in Education
Ofsted is the government body which inspects schools, measures their success, and writes reports of their findings. All Ofsted reports can be found on their website.

Options

Taking place in Year 9*, the Options process is where students choose which subjects they wish to study at Key Stage 4*. English, Maths, Science, RE*, Citizenship* and ICT* are not normally optional. Students can usually opt for a number of other subjects depending on the school's curriculum. There is normally no guarantee that students will be given the subjects they opt for.

Parents' Evening

A parents' evening is an event when parents come into school, sometimes accompanied by their child, to talk to teachers about their child's progress.

Pastoral System

The pastoral system is the mechanism responsible for your child's welfare. Most schools have Heads of Year*, Assistant Heads of Year and Tutors*. In some schools there is a House* system, with a Head and Deputy Head of House. These people are usually responsible primarily for your child's social well-being, although in recent years there has been more emphasis in school pastoral systems upon raising academic attainment.

PGCE – Post Graduate Certificate in Education

A PGCE is the most common qualification followed by graduates wishing to become teachers.

Private Schools

See 'Independent schools'.

PSHE – Personal, Social and Health Education
PSHE is the study and discussion of issues students will encounter in their personal and adult life.

PTA – Parent Teacher Association
Also known as 'Parent Association – PA'.
A PTA is an organisation of parents, with some school staff input, who arrange events for the school, such as fetes or quiz nights, usually to raise funds and generate a social link between and amongst school staff and parents.

Public Schools
Public schools are the most elite and prestigious independent* schools.

RE – Religious Education
Also known as 'Religious Studies – RS'.
Religious Education is a compulsory subject in state* schools.

RM – Resistant Materials
RM is the study of the use of wood, metal and plastics in design and manufacture. The traditional subjects of wood work and metal work now fall under this heading. It is part of the Design and Technology* subject group.

SATs – Standard Assessment Tasks
SATs are national exams students take at the end of Key Stages 1, 2 and 3*.

School Profile
The School Profile is produced annually for parents

by or on behalf of the governors* summarising the school's progress and achievements.

SEN – Special Educational Needs
All schools have a special educational needs department which is dedicated to students with particular behavioural and learning needs, for example, problems with reading.

Senior Management
Also known as 'Senior Leadership Team – SLT', or 'Senior Team'.

The Senior Management are the staff who lead a school. The team usually consists of a Head teacher, Deputy Head teachers, and Assistant Head teachers. The number of Assistants and Deputies depends on the size of the school.

Serious Weaknesses
Ofsted* decides a school has Serious Weaknesses, when it has significant concerns about the institution's performance.

Setting
Setting is a way of organising students into groups according to ability. Setting is particular to a subject area, so a student could be in the top set for Maths and the third set for English.

6th Form
The 6th form is for Key Stage 5* students age 16 to 18 studying 'A' Levels* or vocational* qualifications such as NVQs – National Vocational Qualifications.

Special Measures

Schools are put into Special Measures by Ofsted* if they are deemed to be failing to provide students with a satisfactory standard of education.

Special Schools

Special schools educate students with a particular learning need, for example, a special school for students with severe physical disabilities.

Specialist Schools

Specialist Schools specialise in a particular curriculum area. They have to apply to the DfES* to be designated as specialist, and they are given extra money to develop resources in their specialist area. These schools can also prioritise 10% of their places for students with a particular aptitude in the specialism. Specialist schools are often called colleges, for example, Science and Technology Colleges.

State Schools

State schools are non-fee paying schools provided by the state.

Statement of Special Educational Needs

If a student has significant special educational needs* they may be given a statement which defines what support they are legally entitled to.

Streaming

See 'Banding'.

Supply Teacher
Also known as 'cover teacher'.

A supply teacher is a teacher not employed by the school usually brought in from an agency to cover for an absent teacher.

Suspensions
See 'Exclusions'.

Teaching Assistants
See 'Classroom Assistants'.

TES – Times Educational Supplement
The TES is a weekly paper covering educational issues, where almost all teaching jobs are advertised.

Textiles
Textiles is the study and practical use of fabrics in design and manufacture. It is part of the Design and Technology* subject group.

Threshold
Threshold is an additional salary payment made to an experienced teacher of high calibre.

Transition
Transition is the movement between Years 6 and 7*, the most common point at which students move from primary/junior school to secondary school.

Tutor
Also known as 'form tutor'.

A tutor is a teacher who registers a class of students and oversees their moral and social welfare. They should have a close overview of each tutee's progress, although it is quite likely that the tutor will not teach the students in their tutor group. Tutors are often the first point of contact for parents. A tutor is line managed by a Head of Year* or Head of House*.

Tutor Group
Also known as 'form group'.

In most secondary schools, students are organised into tutor groups. Usually these tutor groups are horizontal – that means they are made up of students from the same year group; less often they are vertical – composed of students from all year groups.

The tutor group is the students' core social group. Students usually register with their tutor*.

Units of Work
The curriculum that students follow is often compartmentalised into units of work. It is likely that a class might do something like one unit of work in each subject every half term. Good schools will assess students on each unit completed.

Value Added
If a school adds value, it means that it has managed to support its students in reaching a higher grade than they were originally predicted. Schools usually use SATs* results to measure how much value has been added. For example, a student with a level* 5 at Key Stage 3* is normally predicted a grade 'C' at GCSE*. If that student then goes on to get a 'B' at GCSE, then the school has added value.

Vocational
Normally found at Key Stages 4 and 5*, a vocational course has a strong work related focus.

Voluntary Aided
In Voluntary Aided schools (many of which are faith schools) the governing body, as opposed to the Local Education Authority*, employs the staff, and decides admission arrangements.

Voluntary Controlled
In Voluntary Controlled schools, the charitable foundation which owns the school, (often a church organisation) appoints the governors, but the teachers are employed by the Local Education Authority*, which is also responsible for admissions.

Years
When a student starts primary school, they are in the first year. When a student starts secondary school they are in Year 7, except where a middle school system operates.

Year 7	11–12 years old
Year 8	12–13
Year 9	13–14
Year 10	14–15
Year 11	15–16
Year 12	16–17
Year 13	17–18

Notes

Notes

Notes

Printed in the United Kingdom
by Lightning Source UK Ltd.
113847UKS00001B/1-48